I0448180

How OJJDP Is Improving Outcomes for the Nation's Youth

ANNUAL REPORT

OFFICE OF JUVENILE JUSTICE AND DELINQUENCY PREVENTION

J. Robert Flores, Administrator
Office of Juvenile Justice and Delinquency Prevention

This Report covers activities undertaken by the Office of Juvenile Justice and Delinquency Prevention
during fiscal years 2006 and 2007 (October 1, 2005–September 30, 2007)

NCJ 223612

U.S. Department of Justice
Office of Justice Programs
810 Seventh Street NW.
Washington, DC 20531

Michael B. Mukasey
Attorney General

Jeffrey L. Sedgwick
Assistant Attorney General

J. Robert Flores
Administrator
Office of Juvenile Justice and Delinquency Prevention

Office of Justice Programs
Innovation • Partnerships • Safer Neighborhoods
www.ojp.usdoj.gov

Office of Juvenile Justice and Delinquency Prevention
www.ojp.usdoj.gov/ojjdp

Photos used in this report: Copyright @ 2007 Alamy Images, Digital Vision, Fotosearch, Getty Images, Photodisc, Shutterstock, and Thinkstock. Photo on page 9 is courtesy of Sonny Odom, The Dixon Group.

The Office of Juvenile Justice and Delinquency Prevention is a component of the Office of Justice Programs, which also includes the Bureau of Justice Assistance; the Bureau of Justice Statistics; the Community Capacity Development Office; the National Institute of Justice; the Office for Victims of Crime; and the Office of Sex Offender Sentencing, Monitoring, Apprehending, Registering, and Tracking (SMART).

FOREWORD

Since its founding in 1974, the Office of Juvenile Justice and Delinquency Prevention (OJJDP) has provided national leadership to Federal, State, and local efforts to prevent delinquency, strengthen the juvenile justice system, and protect children.

While the challenges facing America's youth have varied considerably, along with our responses, one thing has remained constant: OJJDP's commitment to support programs and activities that improve outcomes for youth. This guiding philosophy is reflected in the fiscal year 2006 and 2007 activities featured in this Report.

Among its key accomplishments over the period, OJJDP played a key role in two U.S. Department of Justice initiatives working to rid communities of gangs and combat the online exploitation of children. The Office invested in research and provided training and technical assistance on critical issues identified by practitioners, such as female juvenile offending and disproportionate minority contact. We also revamped our programs serving tribal youth in an effort to strengthen juvenile justice in Indian Country.

To work effectively, we must work collaboratively and efficiently. OJJDP has partnered with other Federal agencies to coordinate programs and increase the impact of taxpayers' hard-earned dollars. And, we have reached out to faith-based and community organizations that share our mission to help children and their families. We have also streamlined our training and technical assistance programs and made performance measurement an integral part of our efforts to ensure that the programs we fund work.

The activities described in this Report are designed to enhance the welfare of America's youth and broaden their opportunities for a better future. We commend the efforts of those who share our commitment to these worthy goals.

J. Robert Flores
Administrator
Office of Juvenile Justice and Delinquency Prevention

ABOUT OJJDP

The Office of Juvenile Justice and Delinquency Prevention (OJJDP) was established by Congress through the Juvenile Justice and Delinquency Prevention (JJDP) Act of 1974, Public Law 93–415, as amended. A component of the Office of Justice Programs within the U.S. Department of Justice, OJJDP works to prevent and control juvenile delinquency, improve the juvenile justice system, and protect children.

Mission Statement

OJJDP provides national leadership, coordination, and the resources to prevent and respond to juvenile delinquency and victimization. OJJDP supports States and communities in their efforts to develop and implement effective and coordinated prevention and intervention programs and to improve the juvenile justice system so that it protects public safety, holds offenders accountable, and provides treatment and rehabilitative services tailored to the needs of juveniles and their families.

Organization

OJJDP is composed of the Office of the Administrator, three program divisions (Child Protection, Demonstration Programs, and State Relations and Assistance), the Office of Policy Development (including the Communications Unit), and the Grants Management Unit. Appendix A summarizes each component's role.

TABLE OF CONTENTS

CHAPTER 1

CHAPTER 1

OJJDP Is
Improving Outcomes for the Nation's Youth: Major Accomplishments

The Nation's young people face many obstacles on their journey to adulthood. At the same time, they have many opportunities not available to earlier generations. One of the principal responsibilities of the Office of Juvenile Justice and Delinquency Prevention (OJJDP) is to help ensure that those opportunities remain available and continue to grow to meet the ever-changing needs of the country's young people.

During fiscal years (FY) 2006 and 2007, the guiding philosophy behind OJJDP's programs was to fund activities and programs that improve outcomes for the Nation's youth. This meant supporting programs that reduce juvenile delinquency and crime, protecting children from sexual exploitation and abuse, and improving the juvenile justice system so that it protects public safety, holds offenders accountable, and provides services—tailored to individual and community needs—to juvenile victims and offenders and to their families.

The Office had many accomplishments in FY 2006 and FY 2007. These accomplishments range from helping the field respond to emerging problems, such as female offending, to using technology to help communities develop comprehensive responses to juvenile delinquency, to working with faith-based organizations.

One of the principal responsibilities of OJJDP is to help ensure that opportunities continue to grow to meet the ever-changing needs of the country's young people.

The Office also continued to represent the U. S. Department of Justice (DOJ) on Helping America's Youth, an initiative led by First Lady Laura Bush. OJJDP's many efforts on this initiative included helping to identify successful programs for Mrs. Bush to visit as she traveled the country speaking out about the needs of America's youth. OJJDP is also especially proud of the role it has played in two major DOJ initiatives: Project Safe Childhood and the Comprehensive Anti-Gang Initiative.

OJJDP recognizes that much remains to be done to prevent, intervene in, and treat delinquent behavior. The activities highlighted throughout this Report illustrate OJJDP's commitment to continually strive to improve outcomes for the Nation's children, particularly those at risk, by supporting programs that have the greatest potential for improving the juvenile justice system and keeping communities safe.

Girls Study Group

Recognizing that the juvenile justice landscape is continually changing, OJJDP strives to respond to new problems as they arise. For example, the Office created the Girls Study Group to learn why an increasing number of girls are entering the juvenile justice system and to better understand how to prevent and intervene in girls' delinquency.

According to the Federal Bureau of Investigation, between 1996 and 2005, boys' arrests for aggravated assault declined by 23.4 percent while girls' arrests for aggravated assault declined by only 5.4 percent. In the same time period, girls' arrests for simple assault increased by 24 percent while simple assault arrests for boys decreased by 4.1 percent.

During FY 2006 and FY 2007, the Girls Study Group made significant progress in understanding patterns of offending among adolescents and how these patterns differ between girls and boys; risk and protective factors associated with delinquency, including gender differences; and the importance of these issues when developing effective prevention and intervention programs.

The study group found that girls and boys experience many of the same risk factors, but they differ in sensitivity to and rate of exposure to these factors. For example, the following factors affect boys and girls differently: early puberty, depression and anxiety, witnessing family violence, attachment and bonding to school, and neighborhood disadvantage.

OJJDP TRAINING RESPONDS TO GIRLS' NEEDS IN THE JUVENILE JUSTICE SYSTEM

OJJDP's National Training and Technical Assistance Center developed the Gender-Responsive Programming for Girls (GRP), a training curriculum to address girls' unique experiences as they relate to their race, culture, gender, development, economic status, and physical appearance. GRP recognizes the biases that affect girls in all these and other areas, such as juvenile justice processing, and is dedicated to nurturing and promoting the individual strengths of girls and their children (if they are parents). GRP embraces rather than stigmatizes the individual experiences of girls and harnesses their potential. The curriculum can be used for enhancing a wide variety of services from community-based prevention programs for at-risk girls to intensive residential programs, detention, and State institutions for girls and young women.

The study group also found that girls in the juvenile justice system are more likely than boys to have mental health problems and to have experienced sexual assault, although some boys in the juvenile justice system also experience maltreatment. The study group further found that girls and boys have similar substance abuse problems.

Although there has been a greater increase in recent years in the number of girls entering the juvenile justice system, this increase may not reflect actual changes in girls' behavior. According to the study group, a number of factors may contribute to the increase.

- Changes in law enforcement policies dealing with domestic violence could be affecting the number of girls in the juvenile justice system. Behaviors once considered "ungovernable" (a status offense) now may, in a domestic situation, result in an arrest for simple assault.

- Family dynamics also may contribute to gender differences in arrests. Research indicates that girls fight with family members or siblings more frequently than boys, who more often fight with friends or strangers. Parents also have different expectations about their sons' and daughters' obedience to parental authority.

- Policies requiring mandatory arrests for domestic violence may affect girls because these policies provide parents with another method for attempting to control their "unruly" daughters.

- Zero-tolerance school policies also may be increasing the number of girls referred to the juvenile justice system for misbehaviors previously handled by schools.

OJJDP anticipates publishing bulletins summarizing the group's findings in 2008.

Online Resource
Detailed information and links to presentations given at conferences can be found at the Girls Study Group Web site at www.girlsstudygroup.rti.org.

Electronic Mapping—the SMART System

OJJDP is helping decisionmakers and community leaders electronically pinpoint local areas of crime and delinquency and target their resources accordingly. The Office's Web-based Socioeconomic Mapping and Resource Topography (SMART) system highlights specific geographic areas of crime and delinquency and nearby government and community resources that are available to help prevent and control illegal activities.

"SMART helped us make sure we were serving kids in distressed areas of real need," said Angela Bussey Perez, the Senior Director of Federal Grants at the National Boys & Girls Clubs of America. Perez advised some 1,800 local clubs to use SMART information to back up their proposals for funding.

Along with maps, the SMART system creates tables and graphs that illustrate a wealth of data about socioeconomic factors such as housing, population, crime, health, and mortality. The SMART system can also help users quickly locate local, regional, and national resources such as YMCAs, Boys & Girls Clubs of America, police stations, and Weed and Seed programs.

The SMART system can be used by a variety of audiences including Federal juvenile justice program managers, State juvenile justice program administrators, gang task force members, local law enforcement agencies, grant writers, and the public. The use of the SMART system is free.

Data sources include the U.S. Census Bureau and OJJDP's Statistical Briefing Book. Additional data come from other Federal agencies, including the U.S. Departments of Health and Human Services, Housing and Urban Development, and Labor, and from KIDS Count, a national initiative tracking the status of children in the United States.

OJJDP has been working on the SMART system since 2005 with other partners, including the International Association of Chiefs of Police and the Mapping and Analysis for Public Safety Program at the National Institute of Justice.

The Office has incorporated the SMART system into its grant application process, requiring that it be used in all FY 2008 solicitations. OJJDP also now requires State Advisory Groups and Designated State Agencies to apply the SMART system when using OJJDP funds to make subgrants. OJJDP grant managers are also required to use the SMART system when reviewing formula, block, discretionary, earmark, and subawards. The Office also uses the system to illustrate to members of Congress where OJJDP is targeting its grants.

During FY 2006 and FY 2007, approximately 3,000 users registered in the SMART system. They included a mix of community organizations, law enforcement agencies, State and local agencies, academia, and national organizations.

Online Resource
SMART is free and available on the Web at http://smart.gismapping.info.

SMART MAPPING HELPS A COMMUNITY IN BUFFALO, NY

The Boys & Girls Clubs of Buffalo, NY, used the SMART mapping system to identify the best location for a new club in the Buffalo area—the Kenfield/Langfield Buffalo Municipal Housing authority complex. According to a community disadvantage index, which is part of the SMART system, this community had a high percentage of people living below the poverty line and receiving public assistance, and a high percentage of families with children headed by females. SMART's mapping capabilities helped the Boys & Girls Club develop the necessary data to get funding for the center.

The club opened on November 19, 2007, offering free programs to children between 5 and 12 years of age. Programs include tutoring, homework help, sports and recreation activities, art classes, drug and alcohol abuse prevention, gang prevention, and more. The center was filled to capacity within 2 weeks, and after increasing its capacity was filled again in another 2 weeks. Buffalo program managers are discussing expanding the center to include programming for teens and would like to start a second center.

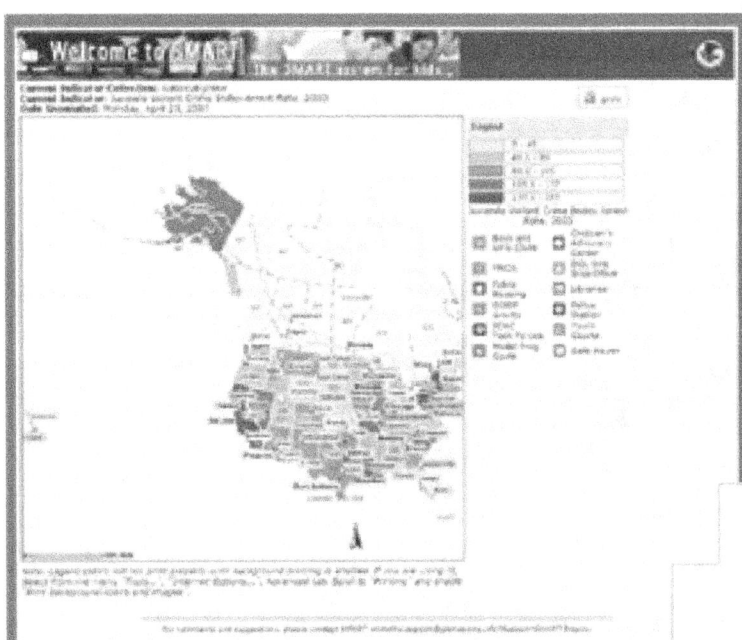

Faith-Based Activities

In December 2002, President Bush signed Executive Order 13279, which created the White House Office of Faith-Based and Community Initiatives. This Order called for a "comprehensive effort to enlist, equip, enable, empower, and expand the work of faith-based and other community organizations." As a result, Federal agencies are developing policies that remove the obstacles that make it difficult for faith-based and community organizations to compete for Federal grants and are expanding the funding opportunities that are open to these organizations.

In FY 2006 and FY 2007, OJJDP instituted a number of policies and activities to support the President's initiative. The Office worked diligently to include faith-based and community organizations in existing activities, sponsored and supported several training conferences to educate these organizations about the Federal grantmaking process, and funded a variety of programs provided by faith-based organizations to combat juvenile delinquency and improve child protection. The programs address a range of issues including mentoring for children of incarcerated parents and commercial sexual exploitation of children. The Office's faith-based efforts are described in greater detail in chapter 2.

Helping America's Youth

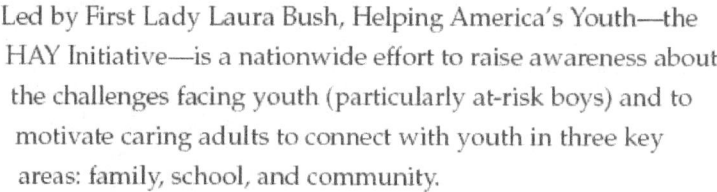

Led by First Lady Laura Bush, Helping America's Youth—the HAY Initiative—is a nationwide effort to raise awareness about the challenges facing youth (particularly at-risk boys) and to motivate caring adults to connect with youth in three key areas: family, school, and community.

During FY 2006 and FY 2007, OJJDP continued to actively support the HAY Initiative. The Office helped plan and participated in regional HAY conferences in Indianapolis, IN; Denver, CO; Nashville, TN; St. Paul, MN; and Dallas, TX. OJJDP also continued to fund and support the White House HAY Web site, which houses the online *Community Guide to Helping America's Youth.* OJJDP facilitated major enhancements to the Guide in 2007, ensuring that both the White House HAY Web site and the *Community Guide* were compatible in design and features. Other enhancements included making the Guide more user friendly, highlighting the benefits and resources of the Guide more prominently, and creating an online "Exhibit Hall" featuring youth-related publications and resources available from participating Federal agencies. These agencies include the U.S. Departments of Health and Human Services, Justice, Education, Agriculture, Interior, Commerce, Housing and Urban Development, and Labor; the Office of National Drug Control Policy; and the Corporation for National and Community Service.

USING THE *COMMUNITY GUIDE* TO COMBAT GANGS

OJJDP's Gang Program Coordinator showed participants at one regional HAY meeting how they could use the *Community Guide* to create an effective community partnership and develop a coordinated and evidence-based response to youth gangs. The presentation illustrated how to implement the three primary steps in the *Community Guide:* form a partnership, assess the community and its resources, and search for programs to help youth.

The HAY Initiative was also featured at the first national conference sponsored by the Coordinating Council on Juvenile Justice and Delinquency Prevention. Supported by OJJDP, the 2006 Council conference, "Building on Success: Providing Today's Youth With Opportunities for a Better Tomorrow," offered a framework for action to address the many issues that face the Nation's youth. First Lady Laura Bush was the featured speaker during the conference's opening ceremony at which time she discussed the HAY Initiative and use of the *Community Guide*.

Online Resource
To learn more about the HAY Initiative, visit www.helpingamericasyouth.gov.

National Conference

More than 2,000 people attended a first-of-its kind national conference sponsored by the Coordinating Council on Juvenile Justice and Delinquency Prevention, January 9–13, 2006, in Washington, DC. Supported by OJJDP, "Building on Success: Providing Today's Youth With Opportunities for a Better Tomorrow" presented a framework for action to address the many issues that face the Nation's youth.

First Lady Laura Bush was the featured speaker at the conference's opening ceremony, and the agenda reflected issues identified in the final report of the White House Task Force on Disadvantaged Youth. President Bush created the Task Force in 2002 to develop a comprehensive Federal response to the problems of at-risk youth and to strengthen the accountability and effectiveness of Federal programs aimed at this population of youth.

Each day of the conference was devoted to a specific theme, addressing research trends and emerging issues; the big picture—what's happening in the field; and what works—moving research into practice.

The conference featured more than 130 hours of workshops, addressing topics ranging from the educational needs of youth in the juvenile justice system to research on the possible links between childhood maltreatment and later delinquency. One of the most popular workshops featured representatives from more than a dozen Federal agencies—including the U.S. Departments of Defense, Education, Health and Human Services, Homeland Security, Housing and Urban Development, Justice, Labor, and Transportation; the Centers for Disease Control and Prevention; the Corporation for National and Community Service; the Office of National Drug Control Policy; and the USA Freedom Corps—who provided information about accessing Federal resources to support State and local efforts to assist youth and families.

Online Resource
Access complete details about the conference in the January/February 2006 issue of *OJJDP News @ a Glance* at www.ojp.usdoj.gov/ojjdp. Click on the "E-News" section.

National Report on Juvenile Offending

OJJDP released a major new report in 2006 that contains a wealth of information about juvenile justice. *Juvenile Offenders and Victims: 2006 National Report* presents a comprehensive account of juvenile offending, victimization of juveniles, and the justice system's response to these problems.

The 260-page, full-color *National Report* compiles the latest available statistics from a variety of sources to answer questions frequently asked by juvenile justice professionals, policymakers, the media, and the public. The Report presents the data in hundreds of easy-to-read tables, graphs, and maps, accompanied by analysis in clear, nontechnical language.

The Report provides baseline information on a variety of topics:

* Juvenile population trends.

* Patterns of juvenile victimization, including homicide, suicide, and maltreatment.

* The nature and extent of juvenile offending, including data on antisocial behavior and arrest rates.

* The structure, procedures, and activities of the juvenile justice system, including law enforcement agencies, courts, and corrections.

The Report also offers the latest information on topics such as school crime, missing children, youth gangs, racial disparity in the juvenile justice system, reentry, and recidivism.

The print report is available free of charge through the National Criminal Justice Reference Service (www.puborder.ncjrs.gov). An expanded online version, which includes data points and PowerPoint slides for all graphs, can be accessed through OJJDP's Statistical Briefing Book (described in chapter 5).

To access the Statistical Briefing Book, go to the OJJDP Web site at
www.ojp.usdoj.gov/ojjdp and click on the "Statistics" section.

Project Safe Childhood

OJJDP is proud to be playing a major role in DOJ's Project
Safe Childhood, which combats the exploitation of children
by Internet predators. The project's goal is to investigate
and prosecute crimes against children committed through
the Internet or other electronic media and communica-
tions devices. The initiative's key partners include U.S.
Attorneys; the Internet Crimes Against Children (ICAC)
Task Force Program, which is managed by OJJDP; the
National Center for Missing & Exploited Children; the
Federal Bureau of Investigation; and State and local law
enforcement agencies. During FY 2006 and FY 2007,
OJJDP participated in the first national training conference
for this initiative and conducted several related training activities across the
Nation. OJJDP's accomplishments in this initiative are described in more detail
in chapter 4.

Comprehensive Anti-Gang Initiative

OJJDP helped launch and continues to support DOJ's Comprehensive Anti-Gang
Initiative, which stresses the importance of Federal and State agencies working with local partners to coordinate anti-gang strategies. The program significantly enhances resources and coordination of comprehensive communitywide
responses to gangs across the country. The initiative is coordinated through the
U.S. Attorneys' Offices. OJJDP's many efforts in this activity are described in
chapter 2.

Assessment of OJJDP Programs

The U.S. Office of Management and Budget (OMB) assessed OJJDP's juvenile
justice programs in FY 2006, and found that the programs were meeting performance goals and gave them an overall rating of adequate. The results were
released in FY 2007. OMB developed the Program Assessment Rating Tool
(PART) to assess Federal programs in four areas: purpose and design, strategic
planning, management, and results and accountability.

For the assessment, OJJDP responded to 25 PART questions and analyzed multiple years of performance measure data provided by the Formula Grants, Title V Community Prevention Grants, Tribal Youth, and Enforcing the Underage Drinking Laws (EUDL) programs. PART also assessed the agency's discretionary funding, which has been almost entirely congressionally directed in recent years.

In addition to rating the Office's programs as adequate, OMB noted the following:

- The programs have developed a number of resources, including an online registry of effective programs for States and localities to promote the implementation of effective practices and program models.

- While additional efforts are needed to make program performance data transparent and available to the public, the programs still compare favorably with other programs focusing on juveniles, delinquency, and crime.

Online Resource

The results of the assessments of OJJDP's juvenile justice programs are available at www.ExpectMore.gov, an OMB Web site that distills information from the PART accountability system.

Performance Measures

OJJDP made significant progress in FY 2006 and FY 2007 in expanding, implementing, and collecting performance measures to determine the effectiveness of funded programs. Recognizing the importance of knowing whether a program works, the Office established measures in FY 2005 for the Formula Grants, Title V, and Juvenile Accountability Block Grants programs to collect outcome data related to the prevention and reduction of delinquency. OJJDP's performance

TAKING THE LEAD

Due in large part to OJJDP's accomplishments in developing its own system, OJJDP's Research Coordinator was asked to serve as the Design Group Leader on the Office of Justice Programs (OJP) Performance Measures Business Process Improvement (BPI) team in March 2007. The team completed a thorough review and analysis of the processes related to performance measures within the Bureaus and Program Offices of OJP. The team's recommendations were approved by the Assistant Attorney General in early September 2007. The BPI team is currently engaged in the implementation phase of this project.

measures require grantees to collect data about the percentage of youth who offend or reoffend and who exhibit a desired change in behavior. The performance measures also require grantees to provide information about whether or not they are using evidence-based programming.

In FY 2006, OJJDP began requiring all congressionally directed, Tribal Youth Program (TYP), and EUDL program grantees to implement performance measures.

To prepare grantees to collect and report the necessary data, OJJDP conducted a number of teleconference training calls and made presentations at grantee meetings. The Office also developed a Web-based one-stop resource tool that allows grantees to report data online. The Web site also provides technical assistance by helping grantees develop a logic model that sets goals and objectives for their programs, select appropriate performance measures, and identify pertinent data sources for reporting on program performance.

Online Resource
For more information visit OJJDP's Web site at www.ojp.usdoj.gov/ojjdp and click on the "Funding" section, then on "Performance Measures."

Training and Technical Assistance

OJJDP improved its program of training and technical assistance (T&TA) in FY 2006 and FY 2007 by consolidating several training projects under one umbrella. The Office's National Training and Technical Assistance Center now provides the majority of T&TA to the field, covering a comprehensive range of topics—from prevention to graduated sanctions to intervention to reentry. The realignment has resulted in significant cost savings of approximately $7 million for the Office.

OJJDP made further improvements by merging numerous consultant databases into a single database, making it easier to find experts to perform peer reviews of grant applications, review OJJDP products, and provide training and technical assistance. The Office also plans to develop orientation training for consultants, to ensure that all the consultants "are on the same page" and adhere to a uniform set of standards.

To more efficiently manage OJJDP-supported T&TA events, the Office also developed a standardized online information tool. The tool allows OJJDP staff to track training activities across Office programs and identify opportunities to collaborate.

During FY 2006 and FY 2007, OJJDP offered more than 100 courses on a variety of topics including child maltreatment, tribal law enforcement, disproportionate minority contact (DMC), faith-based initiatives, afterschool programs, school safety, violence prevention research, and juvenile interview and interrogation techniques. Participants included prosecutors, child protective service representatives, researchers, State DMC coordinators, law enforcement personnel, judges, and treatment agency representatives.

In FY 2007, OJJDP began developing a course expressly for law enforcement to facilitate improved response to policing situations that involve contact with girls ages 12–17 who may be suspects or delinquents. The selection of this topic is based on the results of a training needs assessment conducted by the International Association of Chiefs of Police (IACP). An initial draft of the course was reviewed by a focus group of law enforcement, mental health, and gender-specific professionals. Law enforcement officials are expected to provide further reactions to a second draft in November 2008 at the IACP Annual Conference. Recommendations will be incorporated into the design strategy and tested.

Online Resource

For more information, visit the National Training and Technical Assistance Center's Web site at www.NTTAC.org.

CHAPTER 2

CHAPTER 2

OJJDP Is
Addressing Delinquency and Enhancing Opportunities for Youth

Preventing delinquency before it occurs and intervening swiftly and appropriately when it does are critical components of an effective response to juvenile delinquency and violence. Yet, shrinking resources make it difficult for any one agency or organization to single-handedly improve outcomes for youth. That is one reason OJJDP has been working with Federal, State, local, and nonprofit partners to find ways to access a variety of programs and resources. Such collaboration is necessary, and it is starting to pay dividends.

OJJDP helps coordinate programs at the Federal level through the Coordinating Council on Juvenile Justice and Delinquency Prevention. OJJDP has partnered with many Federal agencies to support a range of youth programs, including mentoring and other activities for at-risk youth. The Office also supports a variety of State and local collaborations, including the Shared Youth Vision, a partnership among several of the major Federal agencies that serves as a catalyst at the national, State, and local levels to strengthen coordination, communication, and collaboration among youth-serving agencies to support the neediest youth and their healthy transition to successful adult roles and responsibilities, and the Federal Mentoring Council, an interagency coordinating body designed to increase the number of mentor-mentee pairs.

Another successful collaboration is the Gang Reduction Program (GRP), which is reducing youth gang activity in four disadvantaged neighborhoods by combining local, State, and Federal

OJJDP has partnered with many Federal agencies to support a range of youth programs, including mentoring and other activities for at-risk youth.

resources. This program has been so successful in the Los Angeles area that the city's mayor, Antonio R. Villaraigosa, invested $168 million in 2007 to launch a similar initiative in another part of the city. According to the mayor, the program is based on the promising results of OJJDP's Gang Reduction Program, which has reduced gang-related crime in one Los Angeles neighborhood by 44 percent.

OJJDP's partnerships are also allowing the Office to reach populations of young people who, until now, were not a primary focus of prevention efforts. One such example is an effort between OJJDP and the U.S. Air Force to prevent underage drinking among those who are attached to the Air Force, either as dependents or military personnel.

These and many of the other activities discussed in this chapter illustrate how OJJDP is helping community leaders, who often think they have no resources, realize they have what they need to get the job done by taking inventory of their communities, reaching out to partners, and working alongside other sectors. With OJJDP support and guidance, these partnerships are helping to improve outcomes for youth.

Faith-Based and Community Initiatives

As noted in chapter 1, OJJDP encourages faith-based organizations to work with the Office and other juvenile justice and community programs in preventing delinquency. During FY 2006 and FY 2007, the Office actively reached out to these organizations and funded faith-related programs ranging from mentoring activities to research projects.

The Office works to ensure faith-based and community organizations are included in its efforts, enhance existing relationships, and develop new joint efforts. The Office also encourages these groups to seek Federal funding for programs to prevent delinquency and promoted their membership in State and local coalitions. For instance, the four community coalitions that comprise OJJDP's GRP demonstration project—Richmond, VA; Los Angeles, CA; Milwaukee, WI; and North Miami Beach, FL—teamed with faith-based and community groups to fill gaps in services for their gang-reduction strategies. (GRP activities are described later in this chapter.) Other examples of OJJDP activities with faith-based organizations in FY 2006 and FY 2007 include:

* In FY 2006, OJJDP incorporated language into all of its grant solicitations that encouraged State and local units of government to consider faith-based and community organizations for subgrant funding and invited faith-based organizations to apply for funding or to seek membership in local partnerships or coalitions, where appropriate.

* OJJDP awarded funds to the National Network of Youth Ministries (NNYM) to develop and implement a campaign to recruit adults to serve as mentors to at-risk youth in local schools, neighborhoods, or institutions. (This initiative is described later in this chapter.)

* In FY 2007, the Office provided continuation funding to the Florida Department of Juvenile Justice for the Faith- and Community-Based Juvenile Detention Treatment Initiative. The initiative brings together local agencies, faith-based and community organizations, and businesses to provide positive, caring adult relationships, greater supervision, and moral leadership to help juvenile offenders in secure facilities transition back into their communities.

* OJJDP, through congressionally directed faith-based and community organizations, has provided safe afterschool havens for youth in underserved communities. These programs offer a variety of program activities that include indoor and outdoor recreation, track and field events, academic tutoring and enrichment programs (phonics, grammar, reading, and mathematics), theater productions, and sports.

During FY 2006 and FY 2007, OJJDP also sponsored several training conferences to help guide faith-based and community groups through the Federal grantmaking process and to build organizational capacity among these groups. Examples of these training efforts include:

- Training conferences in FY 2007 in Denver, CO, and Salt Lake City, UT, featured a presentation by the director of DOJ's Task Force for Faith-Based and Community Initiatives and provided practical information to help States work with religious nonprofit organizations seeking Federal funding.

- During FY 2006 and FY 2007, OJJDP, NNYM, and the Corporation for National and Community Service hosted three training events to assist and challenge mentoring programs to find and recruit new mentors, particularly through faith- and community-based collaborations. Several hundred participants attended each event, which offered information on how to find new mentors, work with faith-based organizations, run an effective volunteer program, and develop faith-based mentoring programs.

OJJDP also supported faith-based several delinquency prevention and intervention programs aimed at improving outcomes for youth.

- The Office awarded funds in FY 2006 and FY 2007 to Big Brothers Big Sisters (BBBS) to support the Amachi program, a national mentoring program that matches children of incarcerated parents with adults who are members of faith-based congregations, usually located in the child's neighborhood. BBBS used the FY 2007 funding to offer mentoring services to Hispanic children of incarcerated parents.

- To reduce and eliminate the commercial sexual exploitation of children (CSEC) and child prostitution in the United States, in FY 2006, OJJDP funded The Salvation Army's CSEC Community Intervention Project. The Salvation Army and its partners developed a national multisite training and technical assistance program to help five cities coordinate their investigative, prosecutorial, and victim service resources. The five sites are Atlantic City, NJ; Chicago, IL; Denver, CO; San Diego, CA; and Washington, DC.

- Team Focus, funded by OJJDP in FY 2007, provides support to boys who do not have a father or father figure in their lives. The Christian-based program offers mentoring and leadership camps during the summer for boys ages 10 to 17. Corporate executives, college and professional athletes, and teachers who have achieved their personal goals speak with the boys at the camps. The boys also participate in sports and cultural activities and job interviews. Team Focus also works with schools to ensure that the boys have advocates

"Most of us find it difficult to imagine the life of a child who has to go through a prison gate to be hugged by their mom or dad. Yet this is the reality for almost a million-and-a-half American boys and girls. They face terrible challenges that no child deserves to face. Without guidance, they have a higher risk of failing in school and committing crimes themselves."

—President George W. Bush

there and opportunities to advance academically, works with mothers and law enforcement officials to help keep the boys from becoming involved with the justice system, and offers parenting training to assist mothers in nurturing and disciplining their sons.

The Office also funded two research projects related to faith-based programs:

* OJJDP awarded an FY 2007 research grant to ICF Incorporated (in partnership with Baylor Institute for Studies of Religion) to conduct an evaluation of the Amachi program in Texas. The study will include both a process and outcome evaluation and examine the impact the Amachi program has on outcomes for children of incarcerated parents and/or family members in Texas.

* OJJDP awarded a grant in FY 2006 to Baylor University to conduct the Religion in Prosocial Youth Behavior study. The research will identify protective factors that help faith-based and secular programs attain competency, develop empirically-based information to help youth resist delinquent and violent activity, and promote an integrated approach to youth crime prevention that includes the role of religion. Researchers also will publish articles on the connection of religion to prosocial youth behavior, review and synthesize religion-crime literature, and conduct a research conference on the role of religion in promoting prosocial youth behavior.

Anti-Gang Initiatives

OJJDP has long supported the use of data-driven, strategic anti-gang initiatives that combine prevention, intervention, enforcement, and reentry strategies. Such initiatives require the collaboration of multiple community partners including law enforcement, schools, social services, community and faith-based organizations, key community leaders, citizens, and other partners. Coordinating multiple anti-gang strategies provides the highest potential for long-term success in reducing and eliminating gang activity. During FY 2006 and FY 2007, OJJDP provided support to local, State, Federal, and (with increasing frequency) international parties seeking information and guidance on gang prevention. The Office's major anti-gang efforts are described below.

DOJ's Comprehensive Anti-Gang Initiative

During FY 2006 and FY 2007, OJJDP played a major role in DOJ's Comprehensive Anti-Gang Initiative, launched in 2006. The initiative, coordinated through the U.S. Attorneys' Offices, emphasizes the importance of working with local partners to coordinate anti-gang strategies. As a result of this emphasis, U.S.

Attorneys' Offices have moved beyond focusing on enforcement-only anti-gang strategies and have begun developing comprehensive communitywide strategies.

The project initially began in Los Angeles, CA; Dallas/Fort Worth, TX; Tampa, FL; Cleveland, OH; Milwaukee, WI; and the 222 corridor north of Philadelphia, PA. The initiative was expanded in 2007 to include Rochester, NY; Oklahoma City, OK; Indianapolis, IN; and Raleigh-Durham, NC.

OJJDP helped develop the initiative and continues to provide funding, training, and technical assistance. The Office provided $6 million (out of a total of $15 million) for the program in FY 2006 to support prevention activities and offered technical assistance to the sites through its National Youth Gang Center (NYGC), which is described later in this chapter.

All U.S. Attorneys' Offices were asked to sponsor gang prevention summits in their districts during 2006. OJJDP worked with the Office of the Deputy Attorney General, the Executive Office for U.S. Attorneys, and the Community Oriented Policing Services (COPS) Office to develop guidelines and make resources available for the summits. OJJDP also provided subject matter experts to make presentations at many of the gang prevention summits.

OJJDP's Gang Program Coordinator also wrote an article, "Gang Prevention: How to Make the 'Front End' of Your Anti-Gang Effort Work," for the May 2006 *USA Bulletin*, which was focused solely on gang issues. The article was the only one in the volume that highlighted gang prevention, and was used as a handout by numerous U.S. Attorneys during their gang prevention summits.

Gang Prevention Coordination Assistance Program

OJJDP initiated the Gang Prevention Coordination Assistance Program in FY 2007 to improve the coordination of resources that support community partnerships that implement two or more anti-gang strategies: primary prevention, secondary prevention, gang intervention, and gang enforcement. OJJDP received approximately 100 applications and made 12 awards of up to $200,000 each for the 24-month project. Grantees are the city of Waynesboro, VA; Alaska Department of Health and Social Services, Juneau, AK; SAFE Haven of Racine, Inc., Racine, WI; New Jersey Department of Law and Public Safety, Trenton, NJ; city of Los Angeles, CA; Montgomery County, Rockville, MD; Office of the Attorney General of Virginia, Richmond, VA; A Better Way, Project Gang Out, Columbia, SC; city of Austin, TX; Leadership Training Institute, Hempstead, NY; United Teen Equality Center, Lowell, MA; and city of San Diego, CA.

Gang Reduction Program

Since 2002, OJJDP has worked to strengthen the reach and breadth of its efforts to reduce youth gang violence. OJJDP launched the Gang Reduction Program in 2003 to reduce youth gang activity in disadvantaged neighborhoods by combining local, State, and Federal resources in a select number of cities across the country. The program received FY 2006 and FY 2007 funding and continues today in Los Angeles, CA; North Miami Beach, FL; and Richmond, VA.

GRP incorporates three new ingredients to the classic Comprehensive Gang Model. First, GRP makes the recruitment of individuals from faith communities and small community organizations a priority. OJJDP recognizes that local churches and charitable organizations will continue to live on long after the Federal Government or large organizations have ended their work. In addition, these local entities often are very efficient, raise their own funds, have existing personal relationships with those in need, and understand the culture and language of the local community. All of this translates into lower costs, faster impact, and longer lasting presence.

Second, GRP emphasizes multiagency collaboration, not only locally in neighborhoods and communities but across Federal agencies as well. OJJDP's work on GRP was made substantially easier because Federal funding was extremely flexible. Funds used in this program came from flexible funding streams at OJJDP and the U.S. Departments of Health and Human Services, Housing and Urban Development, and Labor. GRP grantees can fit dollars to need, instead of needs to money available.

Third, GRP stresses the importance of partnering with the private sector. At the outset of this effort, OJJDP recognized that success would benefit not only those children who did not become members of gangs, but the community at large, including businesses. When crime and violence are reduced, the business community, especially small businesses that suffer most from theft and vandalism, experience significant benefits. For example, the GRP effort in Richmond, VA, has led to large-scale improvements and investments in the physical condition of public housing. Because increased safety, as a result of GRP, has meant more stable tenants and better tenant care of property, the private-sector operator of those units saw an economic reason to contribute to the Richmond GRP effort.

Unlike many previous efforts where communities chose to address enforcement, prevention, or intervention, this GRP effort is bringing all major sectors together and using the strengths of each to address the needs of the communities.

The Urban Institute is evaluating the GRP initiative. A final evaluation report is due in 2008.

The Gang Reduction Program emphasizes multiagency collaboration, not only in neighborhoods and communities but across Federal agencies as well.

Gang-Free Schools and Communities

OJJDP initiated the Gang-Free Schools and Communities Program in 2001 to test a model of school involvement in community-based anti-gang efforts. Four sites originally participated in the program, and in 2006 OJJDP awarded two of the sites, Houston, TX, and Pittsburgh, PA, additional funds to extend programming for a year. OJJDP also awarded additional funding to the COSMOS Corporation to continue evaluating the program. The Office anticipates this will result in stronger evaluation data and findings. A final evaluation report is due in 2008.

National Youth Gang Center

OJJDP established the National Youth Gang Center (NYGC) in 1994 to expand and maintain the body of critical knowledge about youth gangs and effective responses to them. NYGC provides training and technical assistance on community-based responses to youth gangs and is playing a large role in DOJ's Comprehensive Anti-Gang Initiative. NYGC has a network of trainers, training materials, and curriculums that cover a range of topics such as community gang problem assessment, multidisciplinary gang intervention, and comprehensive community responses to gangs.

NYGC also conducts the annual National Youth Gang Survey of police and sheriffs' departments to determine the extent of the Nation's gang problem. OJJDP

WILL POWER TO YOUTH

Richmond, one of OJJDP's GRP sites, launched an arts-centered initiative in FY 2007 that focuses specifically on youth living in severe economic conditions. The Will Power to Youth program, created by Shakespeare Festival/LA, promotes youth development and offers employment training to young people at risk for delinquency and gang involvement. The program helps underprivileged youth explore a work by William Shakespeare and create an adaptation relevant to their lives and experiences. The Richmond Will Power to Youth program hired 20 to 25 at-risk youth to produce, adapt, and perform a Shakespeare play during the summer. Students explored the art and mechanics of putting on a play and the thematic issues that resonated in their own lives while learning vital life and employment skills. The students staged a production of *Romeo and Juliet* in August 2007; OJJDP Administrator J. Robert Flores attended the performance.

Rotisha Hazelwood (Juliet) and Derek Cheatham (Romeo) enact the famous balcony scene.

released findings from the 2004 survey in FY 2006. NYGC has completed both the 2005 and 2006 surveys, with findings to be released later in 2008. OJJDP and NYGC also released *National Youth Gang Survey, 1999–2001,* a more extensive analysis of surveys from earlier years that explores longer term trends in gang activity across the United States. In FY 2007, NYGC prepared an online National Youth Gang Survey Analysis, which includes charts, trend data, and analysis of gang issues.

NYGC maintains a Web site with full-text publications on gang programs and research, a bibliography of gang publications that are not available electronically, lists of gang-related legislation broken down by State and subject, and GANG–INFO, a forum for professionals to exchange information about youth gangs. The Web site also maintains a database of news articles, and 2,500 news articles were posted during FY 2007.

The National Youth Gang Center also published a *Parents' Guide to Gangs,* which provides information about recognizing and preventing gang involvement. During FY 2007, NYGC distributed nearly 300,000 copies of the guide, which is available in English and Spanish. NYGC also compiled two information CDs: one offering gang publications, the other containing information about how to assess a gang problem and implement strategies to address the problem. Information in the latter CD is from OJJDP's Comprehensive Gang Model program.

Online Resource

For more information, visit the National Youth Gang Center's Web site at www.iir.com/nygc.

Growing International Reputation

OJJDP's expertise on gang prevention increasingly has been sought after by the international community. In coordination with other DOJ components, the State Department, and the U.S. Agency for International Development (USAID), OJJDP also participates in the International Anti-Gang Task Force interagency working group. As part of this effort, OJJDP staff has provided training and technical support on gang prevention in El Salvador and Jamaica. Experts from OJJDP also discussed gang prevention at an international anti-gang conference hosted by the National Police of El Salvador in 2006.

OJJDP continued to work with the International Law Enforcement Academy in San Salvador, El Salvador, over the past 2 years. In FY 2006, the OJJDP gang program coordinator gave presentations and helped facilitate training on a gang prevention conference at the Academy that was attended by participants from El Salvador, Nicaragua, Honduras, Guatemala, and Mexico. OJJDP also conducted prevention training at the Academy in FY 2007. The training was part of a larger effort by DOJ's Office of Overseas Prosecutorial Development, Assistance, and Training to work with Central American countries and Mexico to improve anti-gang activities, information sharing, and international cooperation. Participants included law enforcement and prosecutorial leaders from Belize, El Salvador, Guatemala, Mexico, and Panama. OJJDP also worked with USAID on an assessment of gang activity, gang prevention, and community-oriented policing in a community in Kingston, Jamaica.

Other Major Accomplishments

In addition to the programs highlighted above, OJJDP worked on several other gang activities during FY 2006 and FY 2007, including the following:

* In partnership with the COPS Office, OJJDP delivered a two-part interactive teleconference (satellite and Web cast) titled "Preventing Gangs in Our Communities," which was seen live by more than 3,000 viewers. The teleconference has been downloaded by thousands of viewers since the initial airing in June 2006, and is available on the Web at www.dojconnect.com.

* OJJDP developed a Web page that consolidates gang information on activities and resources for DOJ's Comprehensive Anti-Gang Initiative, GRP, NYGC, and OJJDP's other anti-gang efforts. The page contains links to DOJ fact sheets, bulletins, speeches, and other online resources and links to similar program Web sites.

* As noted in chapter 1, OJJDP released the most recent update of the *National Report on Juvenile Offenders and Victims* in 2006, and the Report includes a section summarizing recent key findings about gangs.

Online Resource
For more information about OJJDP's anti-gang initiatives, visit the OJJDP Web site at www.ojp.usdoj.gov/ojjdp.

Mentoring Activities

Mentoring is an effective way to prevent at-risk youth from becoming involved in delinquency and to help already delinquent youth change their lives for the better. Mentoring relationships have been shown to improve youth's self-esteem, behavior, and academic performance. OJJDP has long supported mentoring programs. Besides the Amachi program described earlier in this chapter, OJJDP also funded several other mentoring initiatives during FY 2006 and FY 2007 and supported establishment of the Federal Mentoring Council, a Federal interagency coordinating body whose purpose is to increase the number of mentor-mentee pairs nationwide.

BOYS & GIRLS CLUBS IN PUBLIC HOUSING

A grant administered by OJJDP is helping the Boys & Girls Clubs of America (BGCA) make a positive difference in the lives of children who live in public housing. These children are especially vulnerable to the negative impact of poverty and social neglect. BGCA operates clubs in more than 450 public housing communities with additional clubs in distressed urban, suburban, rural, American Indian, and military communities.

During FY 2006 and FY 2007, BGCA and FirstPic, Inc., established 95 new clubs in public housing. To address the prevalence of drug use and juvenile crime in public housing and other distressed communities, clubs that received FY 2007 funding are required to have the youth in their clubs participate in at least one approved evidence-based program, and to report the results to OJJDP. The clubs can select from a menu of eligible programs, including three programs developed by BGCA:

- SMART Moves (Skills Mastery and Resistance Training) is a nationally acclaimed prevention program that helps young people resist alcohol, tobacco, and other drug use, and premature sexual activities. The program features engaging, interactive, small-group activities that increase peer support, enhance life skills, build resiliency, and strengthen leadership skills.

- Targeted Outreach focuses on youth ages 6 to 18 who are at high risk of delinquency and gang involvement and offers them positive alternatives. The clubs collaborate with local partners to mobilize community resources, employ special strategies to recruit hard-to-reach youth, place targeted youth into appropriate club programs, and monitor the progress of at-risk youth on a case-by-case basis.

- Project Learn reinforces and enhances the skills and knowledge young people learn at school and during the hours they spend at the club. Youth participate in several hours of structured activities each week such as leisure reading, writing activities, discussions with adults, helping others, tutoring, and games that draw on cognitive skills. The program also encourages parent involvement and works closely with parents.

Mentoring System-Involved Youth

In FY 2006, OJJDP developed the Mentoring Initiative for System-Involved Youth (MISIY) for youth involved in the juvenile justice system or in foster care and for juvenile offenders reentering their communities. As part of the program, the Office awarded 4-year grants totaling $1.6 million to four grantees:

* The Boys & Girls Aid Society's Mentor Portland (OR) program provides mentoring to youth ages 10 to 14 who are in the foster care system or have an incarcerated parent. The organization is using the MISIY grant to implement one-on-one and team-based mentoring for 136 youth in foster care.

* Lutheran Family Services of Virginia's Mentor Match in Roanoke, VA, provides one-on-one, community-based mentoring to 20 youth ages 8 to 18 who are in foster care and the juvenile justice system. With the MISIY grant, the organization plans to serve 140 additional youth by 2010. The youth will be recruited through established relationships with the local juvenile court system, social services agency, and Lutheran Family Services.

* The city of Chicago, Department of Children and Youth Services is using MISIY funds to support four community-based organizations that provide

BEST FRIENDS: MAKING A DIFFERENCE

Supporting activities that offer young people opportunities to improve their futures is a cornerstone of OJJDP's operating philosophy. The Best Friends Foundation, a national network of programs for middle and high school students, is an example of this type of program. Its Best Friends and Best Men programs offer scientifically researched and developmentally sound curriculums that promote self-respect and self-control, and provide participants the skills, guidance, and support to abstain from sex before marriage, drug and alcohol use, and violence. The Foundation also offers an environment that encourages the development of healthy friendships, fosters positive aspirations, and supports personal achievement.

Best Friends and Best Men programs are active in 70 schools in 13 cities nationwide—including 21 public schools in Washington, DC, a model replication site. Funding in FY 2007 from OJJDP provided support for Best Friends and Best Men programs in middle schools in Washington, DC, and the targeted replication sites of Charlotte, NC; Clay County, KY; Houston, TX; Martinsville, VA; Milwaukee, WI; Newark, NJ; and San Diego, CA.

mentoring to adolescent males who are involved in the juvenile justice system or are at risk for entering the system. One of the goals of this program is to help youth develop an individual plan to ensure that they are connected to work or school.

- The Mentoring Center in Oakland, CA, serves youth reentering the community from a juvenile residential rehabilitation facility. The center is using MISIY funding to develop a mentoring program aimed at reducing rearrest and recommitment rates among 240 youth ages 15 to 18.

OJJDP also awarded a 2-year grant to the Education Development Center, a Boston-area based global nonprofit, to provide training and technical assistance to the grantees. The first group training for the grantees was held in December 2006 in New Orleans, and a regional training and planning meeting was held in May 2007 in Chicago. To help determine the effectiveness of the program, OJJDP also awarded a 4-year grant to the Pacific Institute for Research and Evaluation (PIRE) to conduct process and outcome evaluations of the program. PIRE has developed and provided each site with a customized outcome data collection package with instructions and a master manual. PIRE also began the development of a literature review that is incorporating the most relevant mentoring research in the field.

National Network of Youth Ministries

As noted earlier in this chapter, OJJDP is working with the National Network of Youth Ministries to recruit adults to serve as mentors to at-risk youth in local

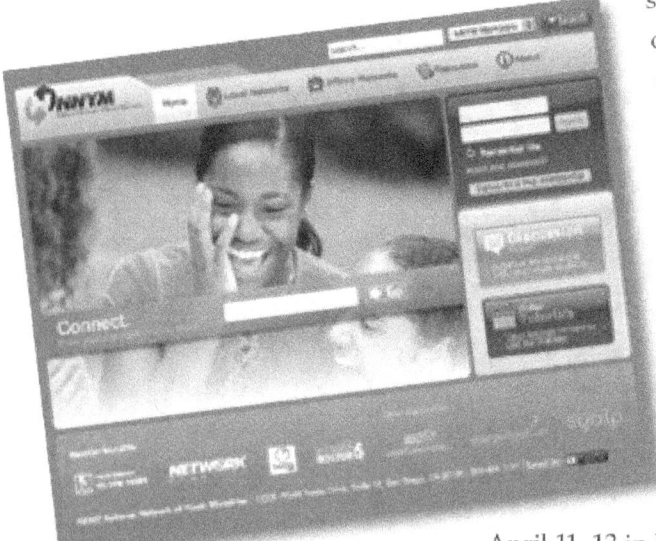

schools, neighborhoods, or institutions. NNYM developed a Web site that provides tools to help faith-based and community organizations recruit more mentors.

During FY 2006, NNYM released a Mentor Recruitment Kit. The free kit includes a DVD, a step-by-step recruitment strategy booklet, and a poster. It can be ordered online at www.mentoryouth.com.

The group also held its first training event in New Orleans, LA, in September 2006. OJJDP and NNYM, in partnership with the Corporation for National and Community Service, hosted two 2007 national training events—February 26–28 in Los Angeles, CA, and April 11–13 in Nashville, TN—to assist mentoring programs in finding and recruiting new members, particularly through community- and faith-based collaborations. Several hundred participants attended each of the 2007 events.

Other Mentoring Initiatives

OJJDP also competitively awarded 10 grants in FY 2007 to support mentoring initiatives across the country. Grant awards range from $100,000 to $1.3 million. Targeted youth include American Indian and other minority youth living in rural areas.

REPORT PROVIDES INSIGHTS INTO FAITH-BASED MENTORING

Funded under an agreement between Public/Private Ventures and OJJDP, *Positive Support: Mentoring and Depression Among High-Risk Youth* addresses the question: "Can mentoring deter high-risk youth from risky behaviors?" and examines the benefits of matching high-risk youth with faith-based mentors. The Report was released in FY 2006 and is available on the Web at www.ppv.org.

Youth Courts

The youth court movement began as a grassroots effort more than a quarter-century ago and has grown to more than 1,200 youth courts in 49 States and the District of Columbia. Since 1997, OJJDP and a number of other Federal agencies have supported youth court programs across the country.

Effective youth court programs (also called teen courts, student courts, and peer courts) hold youth accountable for their delinquency and problem behavior, educate youth about the legal and judicial systems, and empower youth to be active in helping their communities solve problems.

OJJDP sponsors national youth court conferences and training seminars and celebrates National Youth Court Month each September. The theme of the 2006 National Youth Court Month was Correcting Crooked Paths: Youth and Communities in Partnership for Justice. The 2006 national training seminar was held in Albany, NY, and focused on developing and implementing youth courts.

The 2007 conference, Empowering Youth ... Experiencing Justice, was held in New Orleans, LA. The conference marked a milestone for the youth court movement with the launching of the National Association of Youth Courts, Inc. The association is the first private, national organization to represent and serve local,

State, and national youth courts, and the association will work to expand youth courts into an international movement.

The 2007 training seminar in Fort Lauderdale, FL, featured two tracks. The first was designed for individuals interested in establishing a youth court and for new staff and key stakeholders. The second track provided experienced youth court coordinators and administrators, volunteers, and stakeholders with information from local and national experts about what works and about ways to enhance skills and increase their programs' efficiency.

Online Resource
To learn more about youth courts, visit the National Association of Youth Courts, Inc. Web site at www.youthcourt.net.

Juvenile Drug Court Initiative

Recognizing the value of juvenile drug courts, OJJDP developed a new initiative in FY 2007 with the Robert Wood Johnson Foundation (RWJF) to help communities address the needs of juvenile offenders who are substance abusers. The program is based on Reclaiming Futures, an RWJF program that brings communities together to improve drug and alcohol treatment, expand and coordinate services, and find jobs and volunteer work for young people in trouble with the law.

FIRST LADY VISITS YOUTH COURT

In October 2006, First Lady Laura Bush visited the Colonie (NY) Youth Court, funded by OJJDP, where she watched students conduct a mock trial. The visit was part of the First Lady's role in leading the Helping America's Youth initiative. About 13 youth court members and 20 adults attended the Colonie event. After watching the mock trial, Mrs. Bush talked with the students.

"Prosecutor" Matt Bogdan delivers his opening statement in Youth Court as First Lady Laura Bush and other court attendees listen.

INTERNATIONAL INTEREST

OJJDP Administrator J. Robert Flores attended the launching of Europe's first peer panel, modeled on OJJDP's youth court program, at the National Centre for Restorative Justice in England in September 2007. One hundred and eighty guests including United Kingdom Solicitor General Vera Baird and U.S. Government officials attended the launch at Hutton Police Headquarters in Preston, Lancashire.

The Juvenile Drug Court/Reclaiming Futures initiative is helping three jurisdictions partner with States, State and local courts, units of local government, and tribal governments to develop and establish juvenile drug courts for substance-abusing juvenile offenders. The program will enable communities to identify substance-abusing youth, match them with appropriate treatment options, and deliver services through a coalition of providers working under the guidance of a local court. OJJDP is collaborating on the initiative with the U.S. Department of Health and Human Services' (HHS's) Center for Substance Abuse Treatment (CSAT) and RWJF.

OJJDP awarded a total of $1.275 million over 4 years for the initiative:

- Greene County, MO, is applying the Reclaiming Futures model to a pilot juvenile drug court, launched in January 2007 under the Greene County Juvenile Court. The integrated system will enhance and expand treatment services, implement a system of care to coordinate all social services, and increase opportunities for youth and families in Greene County.

- The Hocking County (OH) Juvenile Court, which has been operating for 9 years, is integrating its juvenile drug court program with the Reclaiming Futures model to reduce the number of substance-abusing youth, help them meet educational goals, and increase the number of youth living drug- and crime-free lives.

- The New York State Unified Court System is applying the Reclaiming Futures model to the Nassau County Juvenile Treatment Court program to improve coordination among the Nassau County Family Court and public and nonprofit agencies working with justice-involved juveniles. The goal is to improve the identification of juveniles requiring substance abuse treatment, expand the screening and assessment of respondents in juvenile delinquency petitions, and engage youth more effectively in treatment by increasing the number and range of effective treatment options.

CSAT is providing technical assistance during the first year to support the treatment component, and RWJF is helping sites implement the Reclaiming Futures model. Grantees are also eligible to receive training and technical assistance through the National Council of Juvenile and Family Court Judges. Plans for evaluation are in process.

Online Resource
Information about the Juvenile Drug Court/Reclaiming Futures initiative is available at www.ojp.usdoj.gov/ojjdp (select the "Programs" section) and at www.reclaimingfutures.org.

"Through our partnership with HHS's Center for Substance Abuse Treatment and the Robert Wood Johnson Foundation, OJJDP seeks to promote best practices and the delivery of individually tailored responses that assist youth in taking responsibility for their drug use by enhancing the courts' capacity to integrate the juvenile drug court and Reclaiming Futures models."

—OJJDP Administrator
J. Robert Flores

Enforcing the Underage Drinking Laws Program

OJJDP has administered the Enforcing the Underage Drinking Laws (EUDL) program since Congress created the initiative in 1998. The program has four components:

*   Block grants awarded to each State and the District of Columbia to improve the enforcement of underage drinking laws.

*   Discretionary grants awarded to competitively selected States to support the demonstration of best or promising practices at the local level.

*   Training and technical assistance, with research translation that aids program development and implementation, provided to grantees by the Pacific Institute for Research and Evaluation.

*   An evaluation of the Community Trials program conducted by Wake Forest University School of Medicine and the National Institute on Alcohol Abuse and Alcoholism (NIAAA).

Under the block grant component, each State and the District of Columbia received $350,000 in both FY 2006 and FY 2007. These EUDL funds support a wide range of activities. Many States focus on enforcement, emphasizing compliance checks of retail alcohol outlets. Other enforcement activities include crackdowns on false identification, programs to deter older youth or adults from providing alcohol to minors, "party patrols" to prevent drinking at large gatherings, "cops in shops" to keep minors from purchasing alcohol, and youth-focused campaigns to enforce impaired driving laws.

The EUDL discretionary grant component is supporting several varied initiatives, all aimed at helping local communities use a comprehensive approach to address underage drinking.

*   The Community Trials Initiative, which OJJDP introduced in 2003, is helping communities in California, Connecticut, Florida, Missouri, and New York implement and evaluate best or most promising practices to reduce alcohol availability and consumption by underage persons. Wake Forest University School of Medicine is the evaluator of this effort.

*   The Rural Communities Initiative is helping seven States—California, Illinois, Nevada, New Mexico, Oregon, Pennsylvania, and Washington—implement research-based practices to enforce underage drinking laws in rural communities. NIAAA is OJJDP's Federal partner supporting the evaluation of this initiative.

* In October 2006, OJJDP formed a partnership with the U.S. Air Force to prevent alcohol access and consumption by underage military personnel. OJJDP awarded more than $1 million in discretionary EUDL grants to Arizona, California, Hawaii, and Montana to support partnerships between select communities and Air Force bases in these States to reduce underage drinking.

The training and technical assistance component of the EUDL program has been instrumental in helping communities and States enforce underage drinking laws around the country. OJJDP's Underage Drinking Enforcement and Training Center (UDETC) is managed by PIRE and provides publications, training workshops, curriculums, regional meetings, national conferences, teleconferences, and other services. In FY 2007, UDETC translated two documents—*Guide to Zero Tolerance* and *Graduated Licensing: Two Strategies That Work*—into Spanish.

Researchers from Wake Forest University are conducting the evaluation of the Community Trials Initiative, and those results are expected to be released in 2008 or 2009. Researchers funded by NIAAA are evaluating the EUDL rural communities' programs and the partnership with the Air Force.

One of the highlights of the EUDL program in 2007 was the ninth annual national leadership training conference attended by more than 1,600 individuals. Speakers included Kenneth P. Moritsugu, MD, Acting Surgeon General, and National Basketball Association (NBA) star Shaquille O'Neal, a self-described "supporter of better health for children."

Online Resources
More information on the EUDL program is available through the OJJDP Web site at www.ojp. usdoj.gov/ojjdp or the Underage Drinking Enforcement and Training Center's Web site at www.udetc.org.

"A lot of people don't know that alcohol-related fatalities have risen 11.6 percent in the past year. That's 7,000 beautiful young kids who have passed away—future doctors, lawyers, future NBA players, and detectives. This is an issue we really have to do something about."

—Shaquille O'Neal,
EUDL National Leadership Conference

Targeted Community Action Planning Initiative

In 2003, OJJDP launched the Targeted Community Action Planning (TCAP) initiative to help States and communities develop targeted responses to their most pressing juvenile justice and delinquency prevention needs. This innovative technical assistance program focuses on results, not on process. Sites receiving TCAP assistance must complete a four-step process: make a diagnostic assessment of their needs, analyze the identified problems, develop a response, and implement the response.

During FY 2006 and FY 2007, OJJDP provided intensive technical assistance to approximately 20 sites. The sites are targeting a range of juvenile populations such as potential chronic female offenders, American Indian youth experiencing problems in school, habitual juvenile offenders, and adolescent offenders with a history of assault or aggressive behavior.

The TCAP program is making a difference. It has helped grantees form community partnerships, focus on a specific group of youth, strengthen relationships among stakeholders in the juvenile justice system, and increase information sharing.

The TCAP process even helped one community that ultimately had to withdraw from the program because the community could not clearly identify a juvenile offender population around which to construct a targeted response. Nevertheless, the community's initial planning efforts appear to have significantly improved communication and enhanced systems collaboration within the community.

Online Resource
Visit the TCAP Web site at www.ojp.usdoj.gov/ojjdp.

Juvenile Integrated Information Sharing

State and local jurisdictions struggle to improve the sharing of information by agencies responsible for community safety and the health and well-being of at-risk youth and juvenile offenders. The juvenile justice system and youth-serving agencies often have difficulty receiving the timely and reliable information needed to conduct assessments and determine appropriate supervision, sanctions, incentives, and services for youth.

OJJDP released an online report in 2006. *Guidelines for Juvenile Information Sharing* suggests actions to improve information sharing among key State and local agencies involved with at-risk youth juvenile offenders. Drawing on the experience and expertise of leaders from youth-serving agencies and information technology initiatives throughout the country, the guidelines integrate the three critical components of juvenile information sharing—collaboration, confidentiality, and technology—into an effective developmental framework.

The guidelines are part of the Juvenile Integrated Information Sharing training and technical assistance program OJJDP and HHS launched in 2001. The Center for Network Development (CND) provides the training and technical assistance, and uses a cadre of peer consultants (judges, school administrators, law enforcement officers, and human services directors) to show participants how they can benefit from interagency collaboration and information sharing. During FY 2006 and FY 2007, CND provided training to 85 jurisdictions representing 35 States and territories.

OJJDP also sponsored a national symposium on juvenile justice information sharing in FY 2007. During the symposium, OJJDP Administrator J. Robert Flores participated in a mock talk show presentation with a district attorney and a probation officer.

Tribal Youth Program

OJJDP helps promote juvenile justice in Indian Country through two programs that award grants to federally recognized tribes for activities that prevent and control delinquency and improve tribal juvenile justice systems. The programs are the Tribal Youth Program (TYP) and the Tribal Juvenile Accountability Discretionary Grants Program (T–JADG). OJJDP is also funding research and evaluation programs to measure program effectiveness and to identify resources and needs among federally recognized tribes.

Funding

OJJDP convened several focus groups in FY 2005 comprised of representatives from tribal communities and Federal agencies that work with youth to discuss tribal youth issues. Based on the concerns raised by the focus groups, OJJDP revamped its FY 2006 program solicitation to encompass a 4-year grant period, including a planning year. OJJDP also provided extensive training to the FY 2006 grant recipients, including training that focused on successful community planning. During FY 2006, OJJDP awarded $8 million in TYP cooperative agreements to 25 tribes in 13 States. Twenty-six TYP grants totaling $7.9 million were awarded in FY 2007 to tribes in 15 States.

The T–JADG program provides funds for program reform that hold American Indian/Alaska Native (AI/AN) youth accountable for their offenses. In FY 2006, OJJDP awarded T–JADG grants to the Kenaitze Indian Tribe in Alaska, the Lummi Nation in Washington State, and the Pueblo of San Felipe in New Mexico. In FY 2007, Santa Clara Pueblo Tribal Court in New Mexico, Nooksack Indian Tribe in Washington State, and the Southern Ute Indian Tribe in Colorado received T–JADG grants. Each tribe received $300,000.

Training and Technical Assistance

As previously noted, OJJDP now allows TYP grantees to designate the first year of their 4-year grant as a "planning year." This allows newly funded applicants to request training and technical assistance to help them develop a comprehensive strategic plan and learn how to collect and use program evaluation and performance data during the remaining 3 years of the award.

OJJDP also provides three annual regional TYP trainings for grantees. During FY 2006, OJJDP incorporated the training into its national conference (discussed in chapter 1). The training focused on helping tribes use their strengths and life experiences to develop and maintain programs that are valuable to their communities. The FY 2007 regional trainings focused on strategic planning and included topics derived from needs assessments that the TYP training and technical assistance provider has conducted, and addressed Native American youth gangs, suicide prevention, methamphetamine task forces, and experiential program development, sustainability, and program evaluation.

In addition, TYP joined the One OJP Tribal Justice and Safety Training and Technical Assistance initiative launched by the OJP Assistant Attorney General. This initiative provides training and information to tribal leaders, administrators, program managers, and grant writers about resources available from OJP and OJJDP. During both FY 2006 and FY 2007, OJJDP coordinated its regional training schedule to coincide with the One OJP sessions. The first One OJP session included workshops that highlighted TYP and T–JADG, which also addressed juvenile justice priorities related to public safety in Indian Country, and provided information on available funding and resources.

During a One OJP training session in FY 2007, OJJDP conducted a tribal youth focus group to encourage dialog among tribal youth about their communities, families, and life experiences. The focus group participants—boys and girls ages 10 to 17 from 20 tribes that receive TYP grants—also observed a tribal consultation segment in which tribal leaders from across the country highlighted their community needs. A final report with future recommendations for Federal efforts to assist tribal youth will be available in 2008.

Research Activities

OJJDP is also funding several TYP research and evaluation activities. Six projects were funded in FY 2006 and FY 2007.

* Consulting Services and Research, Inc., is conducting a 2-year process evaluation of TYP and grants funded between FY 2003 and FY 2007. OJJDP will use the information gathered about TYP, its grantees, and the impact of its

funded activities to better serve AI/AN youth and families. The evaluation is expected to be finished by the end of 2008, with a final report expected by mid-2009.

- The National Indian Youth Leadership Development Project is examining Project Venture, a nationally recognized substance abuse and delinquency prevention program that is being replicated in more than 50 American Indian and other communities around the Nation. Although the program, which originated in New Mexico, has been implemented nationally, little is known about its implementation in areas outside of New Mexico. The study is scheduled for completion in late 2008.

- The American Youth Policy Forum is documenting three ongoing TYP activities and will produce a report that provides a clear picture of effective tribal youth programs. The report will describe connections among infrastructure, funding, and leveraging of resources, including volunteers and faith-based organizations.

- The University of Colorado at Denver, in collaboration with the Southern Ute Indian tribe, is conducting a collaborative evaluation of the TuuCai Tribal Juvenile Wellness Court. The court was established through OJJDP's juvenile drug court program for substance-involved American Indian youth on the Southern Ute Indian Reservation in Ignacio, CO. The project is scheduled for completion in late 2008.

- Prevent Child Abuse America, in partnership with the National Indian Child Welfare Association and other partners (Purdue University, Macro International, and key American Indian researchers), is studying the extent and severity of tribal youth victimization and delinquency. The research will increase knowledge about the severity and extent of tribal youth victimization, tribal adult caregivers' perceptions of youth victimization, and intervention/treatment resources available for tribal youth.

- The Pima (AZ) Prevention Partnership Minority Youth Border Research Initiative is exploring why justice-involved tribal and minority youth in Southwestern border communities are at greater risk for early onset of substance abuse and long-term persistence of delinquency, victimization, and mental illness compared with their nonminority youth peers. Researchers will develop recommendations regarding specific service needs of juvenile justice-involved minority youth in Southern Arizona.

Online Resource

For more information about the One OJP Tribal Justice and Safety Training and Technical Assistance initiative, go to the OJJDP Web site at www.ojp.usdoj.gov/ojjdp. For more information about the Tribal Youth Program go to www.tribaljusticeandsafety.gov.

Coordinating Council on Juvenile Justice and Delinquency Prevention

The Coordinating Council on Juvenile Justice and Delinquency Prevention (Council) continued its efforts in FY 2006 and FY 2007 to improve the coordination of federally funded youth programs. The Council has nine members representing eight Federal agencies and up to nine practitioner members representing disciplines that focus on youth. The Attorney General is the ex-officio chairperson and the Administrator of OJJDP is the vice chairperson. The Council meets quarterly each year.

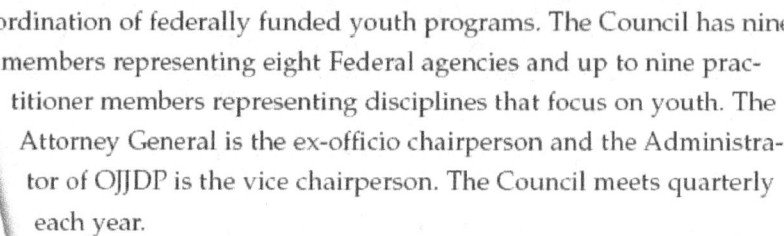

The Council sponsored a successful national conference in January 2006 that offered more than 130 hours of workshops that addressed a myriad of issues facing youth and the juvenile justice system. The conference, discussed in chapter 1, was attended by more than 2,000 individuals.

Council meetings in FY 2006 focused on the following topics:

* The March 2006 meeting included presentations by officials from the White House Office of National Drug Control Policy on drug use trends and anti-drug strategies.

* The June 2006 meeting focused on Child and Family Service reviews conducted by HHS and on mentoring activities.

* The September 2006 meeting provided an overview of recent research and presentations on three critical issues the juvenile justice system is facing: disproportionate minority contact, waivers and transfers of juveniles, and youth gangs.

* The November 2006 meeting was an abbreviated public meeting followed by a closed 2-day Council planning session. The public meeting included a presentation on child death review from the National Maternal and Child Health Center for Child Death Review. The planning session led to the Council's current work under the Federal Partnership Project, which comprises several program and policy tools and resources for Federal staff.

Council meetings in 2007 addressed the following subjects:

* The March 2007 meeting included presentations from a chief judge and education specialist from Louisiana who talked about recovery efforts in post-Katrina New Orleans and the need for services and programs for the city's children.

- The June 2007 meeting focused on partnerships between the U.S. Department of Agriculture's 4–H Program, the U.S. Army, and the U.S. Air Force that serve children and youth whose parents are in the military.

- The September 2007 meeting included presentations about Shared Youth Vision (SYV), a partnership of Federal agencies to strengthen collaboration among youth-serving agencies, and the possibility of using the SYV approach to help New Orleans.

- The December 2007 meeting addressed the disproportionate number of minority children in the child welfare and juvenile justice systems, and included updates on the Federal response to the needs of high-risk youth in the Gulf Coast region.

Online Resource

Information about the Coordinating Council on Juvenile Justice and Delinquency Prevention, including members and meeting summaries, is available on the Council's Web site at www.juvenilecouncil.gov.

CHAPTER 3

CHAPTER 3

OJJDP Is Strengthening the Juvenile Justice System Through the JJDP Act

The Juvenile Justice and Delinquency (JJDP) Act, most recently reauthorized in 2002 and implemented in FY 2004, aims to treat juvenile delinquents in a fair and equitable manner, while ensuring their placement in appropriate facilities as needed. The Act authorizes OJJDP to award formula grants to help States meet the goals of the Act. During FY 2006 and FY 2007, OJJDP worked with all 56 States and territories, providing financial and technical assistance to assist with the implementation of the mandates of the JJDP Act. As required by the Act, the Office worked closely with States to develop strategies to reduce the disproportionate number of minority youth who come into contact with the justice system.

The Office worked closely with States to help them implement accountability-based reforms and to develop collaborative, community-based delinquency prevention programs. These activities are helping States realize the importance of forming partnerships and leveraging a variety of resources to help make a difference for youth by strengthening the juvenile justice system.

Formula Grants Program

Congress established OJJDP and created the Formula Grants Program in 1974 when it passed the JJDP Act. The Formula Grants Program provides funds to States to help them implement

The Office worked closely with States to develop strategies to reduce the disproportionate number of minority youth who come into contact with the justice system.

comprehensive juvenile justice plans and programs to prevent delinquency and improve their juvenile justice systems.[1]

To be eligible to receive a formula grant, a State must address and strive to remain in compliance with the four core requirements of the JJDP Act, which require States to:

- Deinstitutionalize status offenders (DSO).

- Separate juveniles from adults in secure facilities (separation).

- Remove juveniles from adult jails and lockups (jail removal).

- Reduce disproportionate minority contact (DMC) with the juvenile justice system.[2]

---

[1] In this chapter, the term "States" also encompasses U.S. territories and the District of Columbia. Wyoming does not participate in the Formula Grants Program.

[2] In 1988, Congress first required States participating in the Formula Grants Program to reduce the disproportionate number of minority youth confined in secure facilities. The issue was elevated to a core requirement in 1992, and then broadened in 2002 to encompass disproportionate representation of minorities at any point in the juvenile justice system.

ADVISORY COMMITTEE

The Office also obtains advice and guidance from the States, the territories, and the District of Columbia through the Federal Advisory Committee on Juvenile Justice (FACJJ). The Committee is an advisory body established by the JJDP Act, as amended (Section 223) and supported by OJJDP. The role of FACJJ is to advise the President and Congress on matters related to juvenile justice and delinquency prevention, to advise the OJJDP Administrator on the work of OJJDP, and to evaluate the progress and accomplishments of juvenile justice activities and projects. FACJJ is composed of appointed representatives from the State Advisory Groups (SAGs) of each of the 50 States, the District of Columbia, and the 5 U.S. territories. (SAGs are appointed by the Governors and assist their States in developing and implementing the juvenile justice plans their States are required to submit to OJJDP every 3 years in order to receive formula grant funds.) The advisory committee's mandated responsibilities include preparing two annual recommendation reports—one to the President and Congress and one to the Office.

Compliance Progress

Congress modified some of the requirements and penalties for noncompliance when the Act was reauthorized in 2002. OJJDP worked with the States to share this information and assist State agencies with training to meet the new mandates. The Office conducted a series of regional and national training conferences to explain the changes and answer questions, established new guidelines, developed documents, and updated Web pages to help juvenile justice policymakers and practitioners prepare for the legislative changes.

This extensive training and technical assistance by OJJDP is making a difference. All participating States have made significant progress in achieving compliance with the four core requirements. For example, a comparison between baseline violations (based on data submitted when a State first begins participating in the Formula Grants Program) and current violations (based on 2006 compliance monitoring data) illustrates the progress States have made:

- DSO violations have decreased 96.4 percent, from 171,183 to 6,234.

- Separation violations have decreased 98.1 percent, from 83,826 to 1,628.

- Jail removal violations have decreased 94.8 percent, from 148,442 to 7,757.

Compliance rates have remained steady, with the majority of States reporting minimal or no violations of DSO, separation, and jail removal requirements. Although DMC compliance cannot be measured in terms of violations, States must show OJJDP that they are working to reduce the disproportionate number of minority youth who come into contact with the juvenile justice system, and some States are making significant progress in this area. OJJDP's DMC accomplishments are discussed later in this chapter.

In FY 2006 and FY 2007, most States qualified to receive the maximum amount of formula grant funds on the basis of compliance status. (For more compliance information, see appendix B.)

State progress toward achieving the goals of the JJDP Act has been remarkable. However, the hard work of sustaining that progress remains. OJJDP continues to provide an intensive program of training and technical assistance to help States address compliance issues. During FY 2006 and FY 2007, OJJDP made site visits to a number of States, provided technical assistance, and held regional and national training conferences. In addition, OJJDP conducted a national compliance monitoring training conference in 2007. More than 120 State juvenile justice specialists, compliance monitoring coordinators, and other individuals with compliance monitoring responsibilities from 53 States and territories attended.

DSO VIDEOCONFERENCE

OJJDP sponsored a national videoconference, "Addressing the Needs of Juvenile Status Offenders and Their Families," on January 18, 2007. The videoconference, available on DVD, focused on the factors that may lead a status offender to become more deeply involved in serious risk behavior, offending, and the juvenile justice system. The broadcast highlighted programs, practices, and policies that have shown promise in intervening with status offenders. These programs reduce further offending, provide support to families, and steer juveniles toward a positive future. The DVD also features preconference videos on such topics as the family and early intervention, key elements to a successful juvenile offender program, and ways to engage families in prevention efforts. The DVD includes information about Web sites and publications dealing with juvenile status offenders.

To order a copy of the DVD, go to www.ncjrs.gov, search for "NCJ 216888," and click on the shopping cart icon.

DMC Activities

Despite recent improvements, minorities remain overrepresented in the juvenile justice system. Long a leader in the Nation's efforts to reduce DMC, OJJDP continues to increase the scope and number of its resources—including training, technical assistance, publications, and research activities—to help States address this issue. The past two fiscal years, 2006 and 2007, were productive years for the DMC program and included many accomplishments.

The Office released a number of online tools and publications in FY 2006 and FY 2007 to help States make a difference in reducing DMC.

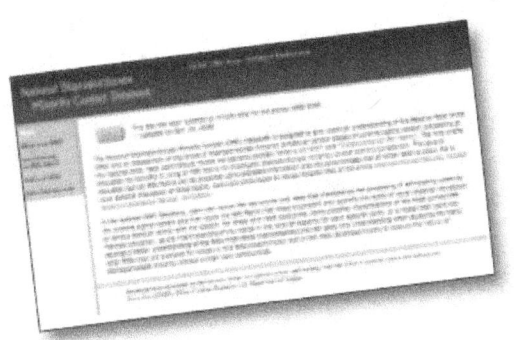

- OJJDP added a National DMC Databook to its online Statistical Briefing Book (discussed in chapter 5). The DMC Databook enables users to review the processing of delinquency cases within the juvenile justice system and assess levels of disproportionate minority contact at various decision points. It includes national data for the 15-year period 1990–2004, which can then be compared with local data.

- The Office expanded its online Model Programs Guide to include strategies and programs that show promise in reducing DMC. The DMC Reduction Best Practices Database includes jurisdictional strategies and single programs that can be implemented to reduce DMC.

- OJJDP entered DMC data from more than 700 local jurisdictions, derived from FY 2006 Formula Grant applications, to the DMC Data Entry System. This tool—available in online and Excel versions—enables local jurisdictions to compare their data with overall patterns from these jurisdictions, thus enhancing analysis.

- OJJDP updated and posted online its *DMC Technical Assistance Manual, 3rd Edition*, which provides detailed guidance on identifying and monitoring, assessing, intervening in, and evaluating DMC. It brings States and localities the latest information and tools for understanding and effectively addressing minority overrepresentation in the juvenile justice system.

- The Office also developed a *Summary of States' DMC-Reduction Activities*, which provides a snapshot of DMC reduction activities. The Summary is derived from FY 2007 Formula Grant applications and includes information on reduction strategies and targeted local sites.

OJJDP also conducted a number of training events and national conferences addressing DMC during FY 2006 and FY 2007.

- OJJDP conducted a 1-day preconference session on DMC at its national conference held in January 2006 (see chapter 1).

- The Office conducted its first DMC Training of Trainers in January 2007 in San Diego, CA. The training was for State DMC coordinators and addressed how to clearly communicate what DMC is, how to measure it, and how to design effective DMC-reduction strategies.

- OJJDP held its 11th annual conference on DMC in September 2006 in New Orleans, LA. The conference focused on law enforcement officers' first points of contact with at-risk and offending youth and on the challenges States face in addressing the Federal core requirement on DMC.

- In October 2007, OJJDP held its 12th annual DMC conference in Denver, CO. It attracted a "sellout" audience of 450 participants from across the country. The conference provided critical information to support State and local DMC-reduction efforts and insights into next steps.

OJJDP also awarded a grant in FY 2006 to the Justice Research and Statistics Association to evaluate strategies to reduce DMC among the juvenile justice populations in two States. Researchers are documenting the steps that Iowa and Virginia have taken to assess DMC, interventions they have pursued, and outcomes they have achieved; and analyzing secondary juvenile justice data. The project is focusing on two localities in each state: Newport News and Norfolk, in Virginia, and Johnson and Linn Counties in Iowa.

Online Resource
For more information about OJJDP's DMC efforts, go to the OJJDP Web site at www.ojp.usdoj.gov/ojjdp and click on the "Programs" section, or visit the DMC Web page at http://ojjdp.ncjrs.gov/dmc.

Juvenile Accountability Block Grants Program

The Juvenile Accountability Block Grants (JABG) Program helps States and communities improve their juvenile justice systems by implementing accountability-based reforms that focus on both offenders and the juvenile justice system. JABG-funded programs hold young offenders responsible for their actions by applying swift, consistent sanctions that are proportionate to the severity of the offense. JABG improves the juvenile justice system by helping jurisdictions track juveniles efficiently through the system and provide enhanced options such as restitution, community service, victim-offender mediation, and restorative justice sanctions.

State JABG allocations were $40.5 million in FY 2006 and $40.2 million in FY 2007. States must use their JABG funds to support activities in one of 16 program areas centered on four types of activities: hiring staff, building infrastructure, implementing programs, and training staff.

During FY 2006, JABG-funded programs served a total of 218,636 youth; 65 percent of these youth were served by a program using an identified best practice. In FY 2007, JABG-funded projects served more than 235,000 youth, of whom 82 percent were served by a program using an identified best practice. In FY 2006, JABG funded training for 19,726 individuals, and in FY 2007, 11,064 individuals received training.

OJJDP also provides training and technical assistance through a number of providers:

- The National Training and Technical Assistance Center (NTTAC) provides telephone or onsite training and technical assistance. During FY 2007, NTTAC trained more than 1,000 juvenile justice staff from more than 30 jurisdictions. Participants included individuals who assist youth who are at risk, mentally ill, homeless, dependent, preadjudicated, on probation, or have incarcerated parents. Training topics included gang prevention, mental health issues, risk and needs assessment instruments, and strategic planning.

- CSR Incorporated manages the Data Collection and Technical Assistance Tool that OJJDP encourages States to use when submitting JABG performance measurement data. CSR staff also provide training and support on the use of the JABG performance measures.

- The JABG Technical Support Center, established by OJJDP with assistance from the Bureau of Justice Statistics and a grant to the Justice Research and Statistics Association, provides States the data they need to calculate JABG allocations for local jurisdictions.

To assess the effectiveness of the JABG program, OJJDP developed a set of performance measures, which have helped the Office, Congress, and the juvenile justice field see the progress and challenges facing the program. During FY 2006 and FY 2007, OJJDP continued to work with the States to collect quantitative performance measure data.

● ● ● **SUCCESS STORIES:** THE JABG PROGRAM

Grantees are addressing a variety of JABG purpose areas. The following examples illustrate how OJJDP and the JABG program are helping local and State jurisdictions strengthen their juvenile justice systems.

● Kootenai County, ID, contracted with Powder Basin Associates for a chemical dependency outpatient program that serves at-risk youth with substance abuse and/or mental health issues and related offenses. Powder Basin Associates provides case management, individual counseling sessions, outpatient groups, and psychiatric evaluations. These services are offered at one location, which allows for timely services, access to treatment without waiting lists, and treatment for youth who do not have private health insurance or who are otherwise unable to pay. As JABG funding has decreased, the county has picked up the balance of costs to maintain the program.

● Constructing a Future in Bannock County, ID, offers a balanced approach to restorative justice for juveniles who are unable to pay court-ordered restitution, probation fees, or detention fees. After completing an interview, juveniles are hired at minimum wage to help remodel old homes and provide other related services to the community. Supervised by a probation officer, the juveniles learn construction skills such as sheetrocking, tape and texturing, painting, roofing, and landscaping. The youths are accountable to their  victims and the community, work during the hours that are most conducive to juvenile crime, and learn valuable vocational and employment skills in the construction trade. Bannock County has assumed the cost of Constructing a Future to preserve the program as JABG funds have decreased.

● The Sixth Circuit of South Carolina (Chester, Fairfield, and Lancaster Counties) created a full-time assistant solicitor position dedicated exclusively to prosecuting juvenile cases. Since the position was created in 2005, the courts have reduced average case processing time in all three counties. In addition, many cases are diverted to arbitration, thus reducing the number of juveniles in secure custody and reducing detention costs to the juvenile justice system. The dedicated prosecutor has established new working relationships with local law enforcement agencies and the State Department of Juvenile Justice to assist in tailoring appropriate case dispositions. He also participates in a truancy intervention program in an effort to decrease the number of status offenders referred to Family Court.

Title V Community Prevention Grants Program

The Title V Community Prevention Grants Program (Title V) helps communities develop a comprehensive research-based approach to delinquency prevention. The goal is to improve outcomes for youth by reducing risk factors and enhancing protective factors in schools, communities, and families.

In FY 2006, OJJDP awarded $56,250 to most States; in FY 2007 that amount increased to $75,250. The JJDP Act requires Title V grantees to garner a 50-percent funding match from the State and/or localities, thereby maximizing the chance of success for Title V-funded programs.

During both FY 2006 and FY 2007, OJJDP continued to work with States to collect quantitative performance measure data. A preliminary analysis of this data showed that in FY 2006, Title V programs served 73,863 youth. Twenty-nine percent of the 545 local Title V programs implemented were evidence based. These local programs addressed a wide range of youth behaviors. Overall, 50 percent of youth participants exhibited the desired behavioral changes in areas such as lessened antisocial behavior (72 percent), reduced substance abuse (57 percent), improved family relationships (54 percent), and elevated grade point average (44 percent). The ultimate outcome measure for delinquency prevention programs is to reduce the offending rate of program participants. In FY 2006, the offending rate of Title V program participants was 7 percent.

According to the FY 2007 data, Title V funds served 56,034 youth. Of the 251 local Title V programs implemented, 54 percent were evidence based. Overall, 54 percent of youth participants exhibited the desired behavioral changes in lessened antisocial behavior (40 percent in the short term and 80 percent in the long term), reduced substance abuse (45 percent in the short term and 57 percent in the long term), improved family relationships (40 percent in the short term and 31 percent in the long term), and school attendance (64 percent in the short term and 84 percent in the long term). In FY 2007, the offending rate of Title V program participants was 5 percent in the short term and 1 percent 6 to 12 months after exiting a Title V-funded program.

Title V Training and Technical Assistance

OJJDP offers a three-part training series to help grantees write successful 3-year delinquency prevention plans. The training includes:

* Community team orientation, which brings together key local leaders and provides an overview of the Title V model.

In FY 2007, the offending rate of Title V program participants was 5 percent in the short term and 1 percent 6 to 12 months after exiting a Title V-funded program.

- Community data collection and analysis training, which helps participants review, analyze, prioritize, and present the data they have collected.

- Community plan and program development training, which shows participants how to use data to develop delinquency prevention plans and how to select appropriate strategies using the Model Programs Guide.

The Office also provides specialized training in performance measurement and evaluation, evidence-based practices, and sustainability. The training is available to Title V subgrantees, juvenile justice specialists, and Title V coordinators.

During FY 2006, 360 participants from 115 communities took part in OJJDP's Title V trainings. During FY 2007, 281 individuals from 138 communities received the training.

● ● ● SUCCESS STORY: TITLE V PROGRAM

The Title V Program is helping make a difference for children in communities across the country. The examples below illustrate the types of programs funded under Title V:

- The Positive Action Program in Shepard, MI, provides afterschool, weekend, and summer activities for at-risk teens from area schools. Other teens are referred to the program by probation services. The program is part of a county effort to provide a continuum of services that address prevention, early intervention, and juvenile justice. Youth participating in the program report improvements in self-esteem, family relations, and positive social behavior.

- The Leadership and Resilience Program in Grand Ledge, MI, is an intensive substance abuse prevention program for youth who are at risk for involvement with substance abuse, violence, or both. The program assists youth in developing leadership skills, improving interpersonal communication, and making healthy, positive choices in their lives. Activities include an in-school probation program for high school students found to be in possession or under the influence of alcohol, tobacco, or other drugs while on school grounds. Since participating in the program, a majority of youth have tested negative for substance abuse and showed improvements in school behavior, grades, and life skills.

- Operation Save Kids Okmulgee is a truancy intervention and prevention program serving students in rural Okmulgee County, OK. The program has been successful in influencing 7 of the 10 school districts in the county to accept a uniform truancy policy. Partners in the project include the county commissioner, the district attorney's office, school personnel, local law enforcement, Creek Nation tribal members, and the county youth services agency. Since the program began, fewer than 10 youth have been prosecuted for truancy out of approximately 2,000 youth served.

OJJDP released the *National Evaluation of the Title V Community Prevention Grants Program* in FY 2006. The online report presents findings from an evaluation that examined sites in six States. According to the Report, since Title V was implemented in 1992, OJJDP has learned a great deal about how communities plan and implement local prevention efforts. In response, the Office has refined the program model and developed and implemented new and improved training and technical assistance activities to support State and local efforts. In addition, communities have become more experienced in implementing this type of planning model.

Online Resource

To learn more about the Formula Grants, Juvenile Accountability Block Grants, and Title V Community Prevention Grants programs, go to the OJJDP Web site at www.ojp.usdoj.gov/ojjdp and click on the "Programs" section.

MODEL PROGRAMS GUIDE

The OJJDP Model Programs Guide is a user-friendly, online portal to scientifically tested and proven programs that address a range of issues across the juvenile justice spectrum. Developed as a tool to support the Title V Program, the Guide profiles more than 175 prevention and intervention programs and helps communities identify those that best suit their needs. Users can search the Guide's database by program category, target population, risk and protective factors, effectiveness rating, and other parameters.

As noted earlier in this chapter, OJJDP expanded the Guide to include strategies and programs that show promise in helping jurisdictions reduce DMC. The additional programs include jurisdictional strategies and single programs.

In keeping with its commitment to encourage collaboration, OJJDP also expanded the Model Programs Guide to identify evidence-based programs that focus on at-risk and delinquent youth. The Office partnered with the U.S. Department of Health and Human Services' Substance Abuse and Mental Health Services Administration, National Institute on Drug Abuse, and Centers for Disease Control and Prevention, and the U.S. Departments of Education and Labor to identify these programs. As a result of this collaboration, the Guide, which served as the foundation for the development of the *Community Guide to Helping America's Youth* (described in chapter 1), includes proven programs that focus on youth problems such as tobacco use, trauma exposure, academic failure, poor interpersonal skills, family dysfunction, social and community disorganization, and sexual activity/exploitation.

Online Resource

To access the Model Programs Guide, go to the OJJDP Web site at www.ojp.usdoj.gov/ojjdp and click on the Guide under the "Programs" section.

CHAPTER 4

CHAPTER 4

OJJDP
Protecting America's Children

O JJDP strives to protect America's children from abuse, exploitation, and victimization. Although physical and sexual abuse of children is not a new problem, access to the Internet has changed the way predators harm children. Families, child protection agencies, and law enforcement now must guard against online victimization of children. During FY 2006 and FY 2007, OJJDP developed significant partnerships with prosecutors and law enforcement agencies to respond to these heinous crimes.

Unfortunately, many of the children the Office seeks to protect live in environments that are not nurturing, respectful, or protective. Whether the negative influences come from live-in partners, abusive adults in the home, delinquent peers, or other factors, many youth simply do not have the support they need to become responsible adults. Without assistance, some of these youth will perpetuate a legacy of delinquency and despair. With help, however, many of these youth can discover a renewed sense of security, worth, and self-fulfillment. That is why the Office also funded activities during FY 2006 and FY 2007 to prevent the commercial sexual exploitation of children and to reduce the negative impact of community and family violence on young children.

OJJDP activities highlighted in this chapter provide a broad picture of how OJJDP is working with communities and law enforcement and social service agencies across the country to vigorously protect America's children from abuse and exploitation.

OJJDP funds activities to prevent the commercial sexual exploitation of children and to reduce the negative impact of community and family violence on young children.

Project Safe Childhood

In May 2006, the Attorney General launched Project Safe Childhood (PSC) to combat the exploitation of children by Internet predators. OJJDP plays a pivotal role in the project, which calls for U.S. Attorneys to organize local task forces to investigate and prosecute Internet crimes against children. Key partners in the initiative include the Internet Crimes Against Children (ICAC) Task Force Program, managed by OJJDP, Federal, State, and local law enforcement agencies, and national organizations including the National Center for Missing & Exploited Children (NCMEC), also managed by OJJDP. (The ICAC program is a network of State and local law enforcement cyberunits that investigate cases of child sexual exploitation. NCMEC is an OJJDP-funded organization that provides 24-hour services on all aspects of missing and exploited children. Both programs are discussed later in this chapter).

OJJDP played a significant role in the first PSC training conference held in Washington, DC, in December 2006. The approximately 700 conference attendees included U.S. Attorneys from all 95 districts, Assistant U.S. Attorneys, and community partners including State and local law enforcement officers. OJJDP and the ICAC Task Forces and other Federal agencies provided training on investigations, prosecutions, and other critical issues. OJJDP also released *Use of Computers in the Sexual Exploitation of Children (Second Edition)*, which details best practices for investigations involving computer evidence. The book is part of OJJDP's Portable Guide series designed to help law enforcement personnel.

During FY 2007, OJJDP conducted PSC trainings across the country attended by more than 200 individuals. The Office anticipates holding an additional 14 training events through 2008 to provide training to all U.S. Attorneys' districts.

To help determine the effectiveness of the PSC initiative, OJJDP also implemented a new data reporting requirement for the ICAC task forces, which are now required to submit monthly reports to the U.S. Department of Justice (DOJ) that track the numbers and types of prosecutions, case outcomes, and sentences dealing with Internet predators committing crimes against children.

Online Resource
To learn more about Project Safe Childhood, go to www.projectsafechildhood.gov.

Internet Crimes Against Children Task Forces

Recognizing that victimization in cyberspace poses a unique threat to the health and safety of children and a formidable challenge to law enforcement, OJJDP created the Internet Crimes Against Children Task Force Program in 1998. The program has created a network of State and local law enforcement cyberunits that investigate cases of child exploitation. The task forces use aggressive investigations, prosecutions, computer forensics, and community outreach to address cybercrime.

In FY 2007, OJJDP awarded more than $3 million in ICAC grants to 13 new State and local law enforcement agencies. With these new grants, all 50 States now have at least one ICAC task force; there are 59 ICAC task forces nationwide. OJJDP also has a robust training and technical assistance program that delivers courses on best practices for prosecutors, basic investigative techniques, undercover protocols, and other highly technical investigative tools to nearly 500 law enforcement officers and prosecutors annually.

The ICAC program has been extremely successful in targeting predators who use cyberspace to entice children. In FY 2006 alone, ICAC investigations led to more than 2,040 arrests and more than 9,600 forensic examinations. Between October 1, 2006, and August 31, 2007, ICAC task forces received more than 18,000 complaints of technology-facilitated child sexual exploitation. Investigations initiated from complaints have lead to more than 2,062 arrests, forensics examinations of more than 9,100 computers, more than 4,700 case referrals to non-ICAC law enforcement agencies, and the provision of training to more than 25,000 law enforcement officers and prosecutors.

A major source of complaints reviewed by ICAC Task Forces come from NCMEC's CyberTipline, which has received more than 350,000 calls since the system was activated in 1998. NCMEC and the ICAC program also collaborated to develop a Child Victim Identification Lab. The computer lab, which debuted in 2006, assists NCMEC in identifying children who are depicted in child pornography pictures and movies.

Online Resource

For more information about the Internet Crimes Against Children program, including State task force contacts, go to the OJJDP Web site at www.ojp.usdoj.gov/ojjdp and click on the "Programs" section.

Commercial Sexual Exploitation of Children

The commercial sexual exploitation of children (CSEC) involves crimes of a sexual nature committed against juvenile victims for financial or other economic reasons. These crimes include trafficking for sexual purposes, prostitution, sex tourism, mail-order-bride trade and early marriage, pornography, stripping, and performing in sexual venues such as peep shows or clubs. The commercial sexual exploitation of children is not only illegal, it brings about significant and, at times, life-threatening physical, mental, and emotional harm to these children. In addition to the PSC and ICAC activities, OJJDP is helping through a number of programs to make a difference for children who are victims of commercial sexual exploitation.

The Office is working with the Fulton Juvenile Justice Fund in Atlanta, GA, and the Office of the Mayor of New York City, NY, to develop model strategies to prevent and address the sexual exploitation of children. Atlanta is focusing on intervention and service delivery strategies that divert victims from the pimps exploiting them. New York is focusing on developing partnerships between police and social service agencies and innovative prosecution strategies for use by district attorney offices.

In FY 2006, OJJDP awarded a $1 million grant to The Salvation Army and three primary partners for a new initiative to reduce and eliminate the commercial sexual exploitation of children. The program is helping communities in Atlantic City, NJ; Chicago, IL; Denver, CO; San Diego, CA; and Washington, DC, align investigative, prosecutorial, and victim services resources to combat CSEC. The primary partners are Girls Educational and Mentoring Services, the Polaris Project, and the Bilateral Safety Corridor Coalition.

OJJDP also supports other agencies that serve commercially sexually exploited children: Standing Against Global Exploitation in San Francisco, CA, which provides outreach and comprehensive health, legal, advocacy, and other support services to these youth, and the Paul & Lisa Program, headquartered in Westbrook, CT, which helps children, teens, and women escape from prostitution and establish positive and productive lives.

In FY 2006, the Office also awarded four grants for research on commercial sexual exploitation of children:

* The University of New Hampshire Crimes Against Children Research Center is collecting data on the numbers and characteristics of Internet-facilitated CSEC to determine how offenders use Internet technology to perpetrate crimes involving the commercial sexual exploitation of children.

* The Illinois Criminal Justice Information Authority is studying the prostitution of children to help develop a deeper understanding of child sexual exploitation.

* The University of Massachusetts–Lowell is working to understand CSEC victims' perspective, to identify factors contributing to the problem, and to determine factors that keep an individual from getting out of exploitative situations.

* The Urban Institute is conducting a longitudinal analysis of Federal prosecutions to determine how prosecutions influence both CSEC service providers and victims. This is the first analysis conducted since the Trafficking of Persons Protection Act was passed in 2000.

OJJDP and the National Institute of Justice convened a CSEC research cluster conference in September 2007 that brought together researchers from projects funded by the two agencies. The researchers discussed common experiences, challenges, and research gaps.

National Center for Missing & Exploited Children

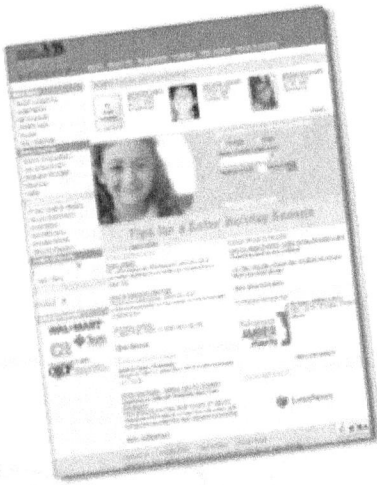

As noted earlier, OJJDP funds the National Center for Missing & Exploited Children (NCMEC), which provides 24-hour services and support to families, children, law enforcement agencies, and Federal agencies dealing with missing and exploited children. During FY 2006, NCMEC answered 131,085 calls on its hotline and assisted in the recovery of 10,754 children. In FY 2007, the Center received 109,004 calls and assisted in the recovery of 11,006 children.

NCMEC also manages the CyberTipline, which allows computer users and service providers to report Internet-based child pornography and exploitation. During FY 2006, the CyberTipline handled approximately 71,109 reports of sexually exploited children. That number increased to approximately 95,000 in FY 2007.

At the request of DOJ, NCMEC rapidly created the Katrina Missing Persons Hotline, a call center equipped with 30 telephones and 160 trained volunteers to take reports of missing or displaced persons from those areas hit by the hurricane. Since beginning operations on September 5, 2005, the hotline has handled more than 32,000 calls and taken more than 5,100 reports of missing or displaced children.

NCMEC also is a key participant in the annual Missing Children's Day commemoration and the AMBER Alert program, both described below.

Online Resource

To learn more about the center, visit the NCMEC Web site at www.missingkids.com.

Missing Children's Day

DOJ annually commemorates National Missing Children's Day in May to remember missing children and their families and to recognize law enforcement personnel and private citizens for outstanding efforts on behalf of missing children. The ceremony for the 23rd National Missing Children's Day was held May 25, 2006, at DOJ's Great Hall of Justice. John Bish of Warren, MA, whose 16-year-old daughter Molly was kidnapped and murdered in 2000, addressed the audience.

The ceremony for the 24th annual commemoration was held May 18, 2007, at the Lansburgh Theatre in Washington, DC. The ceremony featured a message from Tamara Brooks, who was abducted in 2002, and included a video with insights from siblings of abducted children.

WHAT ABOUT ME?

The Attorney General released *What About Me? Coping With the Abduction of a Brother or Sister* at the 2007 Missing Children's Day Ceremony. Written by and for the siblings of abducted children, the survival guide was created to ensure these children receive the support and assistance they need.

The award recipients are listed in the May/June 2006 and May/June 2007 issues of *OJJDP News @ a Glance,* available on OJJDP's Web site at www.ojp.usdoj.gov/ojjdp, click on "E-News" then select *OJJDP News @ a Glance.*

AMBER Alert

The AMBER Alert program, which marked its 11th anniversary in 2007, has helped recover 308 abducted children nationwide. AMBER Alerts are media alerts that are broadcast on radio, television, and highway signs when a law enforcement agency determines that a child has been abducted and is in imminent danger. All 50 States have AMBER Alert programs. (AMBER stands for America's Missing: Broadcast Emergency Response.) The program is managed by the Office of Justice Programs (OJP) with the support of OJJDP.

AMBER Alert activities include annual national conferences—the 2006 and 2007 conferences were held in Albuquerque, NM, and Denver, CO, respectively—and the presentation of AMBER Alert citizen and law enforcement awards at the National Missing Children's Day ceremonies. In FY 2006, OJP and OJJDP also released *AMBER Alert: Best Practices Guide for Public Information Officers,* which describes the public information officer's (PIO's) job responsibilities and provides tips to maximize a PIO's effectiveness before, during, and after an AMBER Alert is issued.

During FY 2007, OJP selected 10 tribal sites to develop AMBER Alert plans, allowing children in Indian country to benefit from the AMBER Alert network. These sites are working to provide tribal children the same degree of protection afforded to other children across the country via the State and regional AMBER Alert programs.

Children's Advocacy Centers

OJJDP's Children's Advocacy Centers (CACs) address the problems of victimized children. Designed to meet the unique needs of a community, CACs are facility-based programs that help coordinate the investigation, treatment, and prosecution of child abuse cases. Recognizing that child abuse is a multifaceted problem, CACs involve multidisciplinary teams of professionals—child protective and victim advocacy services, medical and mental health agencies, and law enforcement and prosecution—to provide a continuum of services to victims and nonoffending family members. Working together, these professionals gain a more complete understanding of each case, allowing them to identify the most effective response.

One of the primary goals of the CAC program is to ensure that child abuse victims are not further traumatized by the systems designed to protect them. By developing a comprehensive and appropriate response to child abuse, CACs can help minimize the trauma to children who, in addition to dealing with the physical, emotional, and psychological effects of their abuse, may need to serve as witnesses in criminal prosecutions or be placed in alternate home settings.

OJJDP supports Regional CACs in the Midwest, Northeast, South, and West. These centers encourage communities to establish local CACs and provide existing CACs with training, technical assistance, and other services. OJJDP also supports the National Children's Alliance, a nonprofit organization that provides services to local CACs.

An OJJDP-funded study conducted by the University of New Hampshire's Crimes Against Children Research Center evaluated the impact of CACs on children, families, systems, and communities. Researchers gathered data on more than 1,000 cases of child sexual abuse from four CACs and from comparison communities without CACs. The study's findings, released in 2006, highlighted some of the benefits of CACs:

- **Coordination of investigations:** Police in CAC communities were involved in 81 percent of child protective services investigations of sexual abuse, compared to 52 percent in other communities. Team interviews (two or more observers) were more common in CAC cases (28 percent) than non-CAC cases (6 percent).

- **Medical exams:** In the CAC sample, nearly half (48 percent) of child victims received a forensic medical examination, compared to less than a fourth (21 percent) of non-CAC cases.

- **Mental health services:** Sixty percent of CAC children received referrals for mental health services compared to 22 percent in non-CAC communities. Of the CAC children referred, 31 percent were counseled onsite by a therapist specializing in treatment of child abuse victims.

Online Resource

For information on Children's Advocacy Centers, including the locations of the Regional Centers, go to the OJJDP Web site at www.ojp.usdoj.gov/ojjdp and click on the "Programs" section. Read about the national evaluation of CACs at www.unh.edu/ccrc/multi-site_evaluation_children.html.

INTERNATIONAL RECOGNITION

The OJJDP Administrator and several OJJDP grantees involved with the CAC program spoke at the 16th International Congress on Child Abuse and Neglect held in York, England, in September 2006. More than 1,000 representatives from 80 countries attended the meeting. CACs have been growing internationally and are under development in Canada, Iceland, Poland, and Sweden.

Publications

In addition to the documents discussed throughout this chapter, OJJDP released a number of other publications in FY 2006 and FY 2007 designed to help protect America's children.

The Office reprinted several of its popular Portable Guides, a series of documents that provide practical information on investigating child abuse and neglect. Written by nationally recognized experts, the Guides are presented in a user-friendly format for quick on-the-job reference by police officers and detectives. The Guides are also useful for social workers, physicians, attorneys, and others on the frontlines of reporting, investigating, and prosecuting crimes against children. The series includes 14 titles, each addressing a specific topic. OJJDP released reprints of the following Guides in FY 2006:

- *Criminal Investigation of Child Sexual Abuse.*

- *Interviewing Child Witnesses and Victims of Sexual Abuse.*

- *Photodocumentation in the Investigation of Child Abuse.*

- *Recognizing When a Child's Injury or Illness Is Caused by Abuse.*

- *Use of Computers in the Sexual Exploitation of Children, Second Edition.*

The Office also updated and published *A Family Resource Guide on International Parental Kidnapping.* The Guide includes important developments in policy and practice since the first edition was published in 2002. OJJDP also released the fifth edition of *Federal Resources on Missing and Exploited Children: A Directory for Law Enforcement and Other Public and Private Agencies* in FY 2007.

Safe Start Initiative

The Safe Start Initiative is a four-part project funded by OJJDP to prevent and reduce the negative impact of family and community violence on young children. The initiative is expanding partnerships among family- and youth-serving agencies such as early childhood education/development, health, mental health, child welfare, family support, substance abuse prevention/intervention, domestic violence/crisis intervention, law enforcement, the courts, and legal services.

Each tier of the Safe Start Initiative was designed with a specific goal.

* Phase I expanded the system of care to children exposed to violence.

* Phase II is identifying what works and what doesn't in lessening and preventing the harmful effects of exposure.

* Phase III will build a research base of effective strategies to address children's exposure to violence.

* Phase IV will promote the adoption and use of these strategies across the Nation.

The first phase of the initiative, the Safe Start Demonstration Project (SSDP), provided funding to 11 diverse sites (urban, rural, and tribal communities) and has been completed. SSDP created a comprehensive system that improved access, delivery, and quality of services for young children exposed to violence and their families. The communities expanded existing partnerships among law enforcement, mental health, domestic violence, and child welfare agencies, and family and dependency courts.

An evaluation of the 11 sites conducted by the Association for the Study and Development of Communities found that four factors improve outcomes for children exposed to violence: expanding existing partnerships and implementing system-change activities, creating coordinated and comprehensive systems of care, institutionalizing system changes, and increasing community support.

The second phase, the Safe Start Promising Approaches component, began in FY 2005 when OJJDP awarded grants to 15 communities to pilot, test, and evaluate innovative intervention practices. This phase is building knowledge about the effectiveness of evidence-based, promising programs intended to reduce the harmful effects of children's exposure to violence.

The RAND Corporation is conducting an OJJDP-funded outcome evaluation of this second wave of communities. Researchers are examining program outcomes, startup and implementation processes, and training needs. The results will be used to develop an evidence base of promising practices and policies that yield the best outcomes for children exposed to violence and their families, and will be widely disseminated so other communities can replicate promising practices. Initial findings indicate that recruiting families for the program is a challenge, community buy-in is difficult, and research requirements are burdensome for grantees.

OJJDP is also funding a National Study of Children's Exposure to Violence. The research, which is being conducted by the University of New Hampshire, Crimes Against Children Research Center, is examining a number of issues including:

* How rates of exposure to violence vary across demographic characteristics, such as gender, race, age, and family structure.

* The characteristics of individual cases of violence exposure, such as the severity of the event and the child's relationship to the perpetrator.

* The extent to which children disclose incidents of violence to various individuals and, when applicable, the nature and source of assistance or treatment given to the child.

OJJDP also supports the Safe Start Center, which provides training and technical assistance to the Safe Start communities. Center activities include conducting national teleconferences and recruiting and developing a national database of consultants with specific technical and content expertise. The Center also convenes national and regional Safe Start meetings to disseminate information to grantees, national partners, and the field.

Online Resources
For more information on the Safe Start initiative, go to the OJJDP Web site at www.ojp.usdoj.gov/ojjdp and click on the "Programs" section. Additional information is available on the Safe Start Center Web site at www.safestartcenter.org.

HOW THE JUSTICE SYSTEM RESPONDS TO JUVENILE VICTIMS

OJJDP released *How the Justice System Responds to Juvenile Victims: A Comprehensive Model* in FY 2006. Part of the Crimes Against Children Series, this Bulletin introduces the concept of a juvenile victim justice system. The Bulletin identifies the major elements of this system by delineating how cases move through it, reviewing each step for the child protection and criminal justice systems, and describing the interaction of the agencies and individuals involved.

CHAPTER 5

CHAPTER 5

OJJDP Is
Keeping the Nation Informed

OJJDP has a responsibility to keep the Nation informed about pressing juvenile justice issues and promising programs to address them. The Office also has a responsibility to provide information to help policymakers and practitioners replicate programs and strategies deemed effective on the basis of stringent, research-based criteria.

During FY 2006 and FY 2007, OJJDP used a number of dissemination vehicles to keep the field informed. OJJDP research projects were discussed at several conferences. The Office also used electronic publishing, which keeps costs down and makes it possible to update statistical information soon after data become available. The Office also published a number of statistical and research publications, highlighted throughout this Report. The activities described in this chapter are helping keep the Nation informed about critical juvenile justice issues and possible approaches to solve them.

Sharing Research Findings

OJJDP's research activities provide valuable information about many critical issues facing practitioners and policymakers. The Office recognizes that these findings need to be widely disseminated if they are to be used to improve outcomes for the Nation's children. In addition to online

OJJDP is keeping the Nation informed about critical juvenile justice issues and possible approaches to solve them.

and published information, the Office shared these findings with the field through two important venues during FY 2006 and FY 2007:

NIJ Conference

OJJDP helped organize several juvenile justice research panels for the annual National Institute of Justice (NIJ) conference in FY 2007. The conference brought together Federal, State, and local criminal justice scholars, policymakers, and practitioners to share the latest information on research findings and technological advances. The juvenile justice panels discussed findings from a number of OJJDP research studies.

- "Disproportionate Minority Contact (DMC): Competing Causal Arguments and Remedies" reviewed research on the sources of disproportionate representation of minority youth in the juvenile justice system and approaches to reducing DMC.

- "In Search of Evidence-Based Practices in Juvenile Corrections" presented evaluation results from STREETSmart, a reentry program that provides job placement, continuing education, and mentoring to assist youth leaving the Florida Department of Juvenile Justice's Avon Park Youth Academy.

- "Recent Findings From OJJDP's Causes and Correlates Program of Research" highlighted the latest findings from three coordinated longitudinal research projects designed to improve understanding of serious delinquency, violence, and drug use. OJJDP has supported this research since 1986.

Panels also discussed findings from OJJDP's Girls Study Group (see chapter 1) and findings from the annual National Youth Gang Surveys (see chapter 2).

Online Resource
For additional information about the conference, visit www.ojp.usdoj.gov/nij/events/ nij_conference/welcome.html.

ASC Annual Meeting

OJJDP staff and grantees also discussed many OJJDP-funded research programs at the American Society of Criminology (ASC) annual meeting in November 2007. In addition to discussions about the Girls Study Group and OJJDP's Gang Reduction Program, the following OJJDP programs were highlighted:

- **Commercial Sexual Exploitation of Children and Youth.** Panelists discussed OJJDP-funded studies on how this crime can be detected and its victims protected. Presentations included findings from an analysis of Federal commercial sexual exploitation of children prosecutions since the Trafficking Victims Protection Act of 2000 was passed.

- **The Safe Schools/Healthy Students Initiative.** This is a landmark collaboration supported by the U.S. Departments of Justice, Education, and Health and Human Services. Researchers shared findings from a cross-site evaluation of the program and discussed school and classroom climate, school violence and safety, and student substance use.

- **Injuries in Juvenile Corrections and Detention Facilities.** This study is part of OJJDP's Performance-based Standards (PbS) for Youth Corrections and Detention Facilities project. Researchers are analyzing data from six PbS facilities and examining institutional and individual factors that play a role in injuries in secure juvenile facilities.

Statistical Briefing Book

The Statistical Briefing Book (SBB) section of OJJDP's Web site provides a wealth of information for practitioners, policymakers, the media, and the public. This online tool has current statistics about juvenile crime and victimization and about youth involved in the juvenile justice system. SBB is especially reliable because data are continually updated, ensuring that users receive timely information. SBB includes a Frequently Asked Questions section, publications, data analysis tools, and national data sets.

OJJDP made many enhancements to SBB during FY 2006 and FY 2007. A major achievement was the creation of an expanded online version of *Juvenile Offenders and Victims: 2006 National Report.* This user-friendly online resource presents the full report and individual chapters in PDF format and includes an overview of the report, content summaries for individual chapters, and statistical highlights. It also includes Excel tables that present data points for graphs and Powerpoint presentations of graphs and maps.

Other major additions and updates to SBB include:

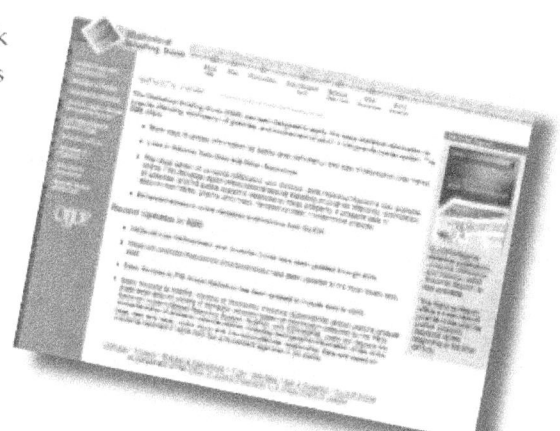

* A National Disproportionate Minority Contact (DMC) Databook that enables users to review the processing of delinquency cases within the juvenile justice system and assess levels of DMC at various decision points. The Databook includes national data for the 15-year period 1990–2004, which can be compared with local data.

* The Juvenile Court Statistics Databook, which provides convenient access to national estimates of the more than 30 million delinquency cases processed by the Nation's juvenile courts between 1985 and 2004. Users can view preformatted tables that describe the demographic characteristics of youth involved in the juvenile justice system and how juvenile courts process these cases.

* Easy Access to FBI's Supplementary Homicide Reports: 1980–2005 has been updated with data through 2005.

* Easy Access to State and County Juvenile Court Case Counts has been updated with data through 2004.

* The Census of Juveniles in Residential Placement Databook, which provides access to national and State data about the characteristics of juvenile offenders in residential placement facilities, has been updated to include information from the 2006 census.

SBB has become a primary source of information on juvenile crime and juvenile justice for individuals within the United States and throughout the world. During FY 2006, SBB received 15,655,835 hits; that number rose to 16,064,074 in FY 2007.

Online Resource
To access the Statistical Briefing Book, go to the OJJDP Web site at www.ojp.usdoj.gov/ojjdp and click on the "Statistics" section.

OJJDP Web Site

OJJDP's Web site remains the Office's primary vehicle for keeping policymakers and the public informed about its work and about juvenile justice issues. OJJDP uses the latest technology to ensure that the Web site is current and easily accessible and navigable by users. Information is targeted at specific audiences, including first-time users, students looking for research information, users seeking funding information or statistics, policymakers, and practitioners.

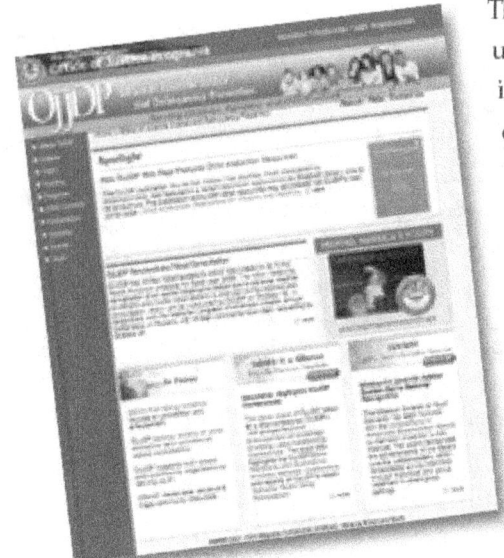

The heart of the Web site is its database-driving capability, which gives users quick access to comprehensive information. For example, by visiting the "Topics" page and selecting a specific topic or subtopic, users can access all items related to that subject area, such as funding opportunities, programs, events, and publications.

In keeping with its commitment to collaborate with other government agencies and youth-serving organizations, the Web page disseminates timely information about these organizations' meetings, grant opportunities, and publications. The OJJDP Web site also is a prime source of information about President Bush's Helping America's Youth Initiative, which is led by First Lady Laura Bush, and about DOJ's many gang initiatives.

The importance of OJJDP's Web site as a leading information resource on juvenile justice and related topics continues to grow. As more people look to the Web site as a dependable source of relevant information, the number of hits it has received has risen steadily over the past two fiscal years—from less than 49 million in FY 2005 to more than 52 million in FY 2007.

The Web site unveiled a new design in 2007, with a royal blue background that complements the new OJP banner above it. The banner allows visitors easier access to the resources of OJJDP's sister agencies within OJP, and the new design is the first of several improvements to the OJJDP Web site that are planned.

Electronic Newsletter

Another popular online information tool is *OJJDP News @ a Glance*. This bimonthly newsletter is sent to subscribers via e-mail and is also available on the Web site. With an emphasis on electronic dissemination, the newsletter highlights major OJJDP activities, grant solicitations and awards, new publications, and conferences. A special e-mail feature makes it easy to share an issue with a colleague, and users also can access a printer-friendly version of the newsletter. Subscribership has more than doubled over the past two fiscal years—from 10,346 at the close of FY 2005 to 22,372 for FY 2007, a substantial increase of 116 percent.

JUVJUST

OJJDP's electronic listserv, JUVJUST, provides e-mail notices of timely information on juvenile justice and other youth service-related news. JUVJUST subscribers receive weekly announcements about publications, funding opportunities, conferences, and other valuable resources, and these postings are the perfect complement to the bimonthly newsletter. OJJDP has sent out as many as 20 JUVJUST announcements a month. The number of individuals enrolled to receive these announcements has grown from 14,275 at the end of FY 2005 to 17,606 for FY 2007, an increase of 23 percent.

Online Resource

To subscribe to *OJJDP News @ a Glance* and JUVJUST announcements, go to the OJJDP Web page at www.ojp.usdoj.gov/ojjdp and click on the appropriate "Subscribe" button on the home page. Both services are free.

Juvenile Court Statistics

OJJDP funds the National Juvenile Court Data Archive (Archive), which provides information about cases handled by courts with juvenile jurisdiction. OJJDP established the Archive at the National Center for Juvenile Justice (NCJJ) to provide automated juvenile court data sets to assist researchers and policymakers. In addition to the online SBB (described earlier in this chapter), NCJJ produces several annual statistical reports for OJJDP based on Archive data.

Juvenile Court Statistics, 2003–2004 is the latest edition in one of the Nation's oldest justice statistical publications, dating back to 1920. Released in FY 2007, this edition profiles more than 1.6 million delinquency cases handled by courts with juvenile jurisdiction in 2002 and describes trends since 1985. The report includes State and county data for both 2001 and 2002, and focuses on cases involving juveniles charged with law violations (delinquency or status offenses). The data used in the analyses were contributed to the Archive by nearly 1,900 courts that had jurisdiction over more than 77 percent of the juvenile population in 2004. The report is available only online.

OJJDP also released three online Fact Sheets in FY 2006 that highlight selected statistics from the Archive:

* *Delinquency Cases in Juvenile Court, 2002* summarizes statistics on the size and characteristics of the juvenile court delinquency caseload in 2002.

* *Person Offenses in Juvenile Court, 1985–2002* summarizes statistics on person offense cases handled by juvenile courts in 2002 and notes trends from 1985.

- *Juvenile Delinquency Probation Caseload, 1985–2002* summarizes statistics on the juvenile delinquency probation caseload in 2002 and notes trends from 1985.

Other Publications

In addition to the publications discussed above and throughout this annual report, OJJDP published a number of other important publications in FY 2006 and FY 2007.

- *Juvenile Arrests 2004* summarizes and analyzes national and State juvenile arrest data presented in the FBI report *Crime in the United States, 2004*. The Bulletin reports that the juvenile violent crime arrest rate in 2004 reached its lowest level since 1980. The juvenile arrest rate for each of the offenses tracked in the FBI's Violent Crime Index (murder, forcible rape, robbery, and aggravated assault) has been declining steadily since the mid-1990s; the murder rate declined 77 percent from its 1993 peak through 2004.

- *Lessons Learned From Safe Kids/Safe Streets* discusses the experiences of five sites implementing Safe Kids/Safe Streets projects, which seek to break the cycle of early child maltreatment and subsequent behavioral problems. The experiences discussed in the Bulletin offer considerable insight into collaboration building, systems reform, service options, and other strategies.

- *Psychiatric Disorders of Youth in Detention* draws on research conducted by the Northwestern Juvenile Project, which measured the prevalence of alcohol, drug, and mental disorders among youth detained at the Cook County Juvenile Temporary Detention Center in Illinois.

- *Federal Advisory Committee on Juvenile Justice Annual Report* outlines critical concerns and issues identified by FACJJ members and presents recommendations for improving the juvenile justice system. During FY 2006 and FY 2007, OJJDP released the 2005, 2006, and 2007 FACJJ annual reports.

Truancy Toolkit

In FY 2007, OJJDP released an online resource for communities interested in instituting a program to reduce truancy. The Toolkit for Creating Your Own Truancy Reduction Program provides comprehensive information and resources to guide communities, schools, and parents in addressing the problem of truancy.

JUVENILES IN CUSTODY

Since OJJDP's inception, an important part of its information dissemination role has been to gather and report data on youth held in public and private juvenile custody facilities. The Census of Juveniles in Residential Placement (CJRP) and the Juvenile Residential Facility Census (JRFC), administered by OJJDP in alternate years, provide comprehensive data on juveniles in custody and the facilities that house them. In addition, the Survey of Youth in Residential Placement asks youth about their background and experiences. This section highlights key findings primarily from the 2006 CJRP and briefly summarizes information on deaths of juveniles in custody.

Characteristics of the Juvenile Custody Population

The biennial CJRP provides a 1-day "snapshot" of youth held in public and private juvenile detention and correctional facilities, including offense, gender, race, age, and other data. The following highlights are primarily from the census conducted on February 22, 2006.

Overview

- Nearly 93,000 youth—295 per 100,000 youth in the general population—were held in juvenile residential placement facilities on the 2006 census date. Of this number, 88,137 were held for delinquency offenses, and 4,717 for status offenses.

- About a third of the youth in custody had been placed in a facility by a juvenile court judge because they had committed a person offense, and about a quarter had committed a property offense. The most common delinquent offenses were assault and burglary. The most common status offense was ungovernability.

- For most offenses, fewer juveniles were held in 2006 than in 2001.

Gender and Age

Although males dominate the juvenile custody population, the female proportion has grown over the years.

- Nearly 14,000 female juvenile offenders were in custody on the 2006 census date—comprising 15 percent of all offenders held.

- Between 1997 and 2006, the number of female juveniles in custody decreased 2 percent, compared with 13 percent for males. The number of female delinquent offenders increased 9 percent while the number of male delinquent offenders decreased 13 percent. The number of status offenders in custody decreased 40 percent for females, and 23 percent for males.

- Female juvenile offenders in custody tend to be a bit younger than their male counterparts. In 2006, juveniles age 15 or younger accounted for 42 percent of females in custody, compared with 32 percent of males. The most common age was 16 for both females and males.

Race

Nonwhite youth account for the majority of juveniles in custody.

* More than 60,000 minority youth were held in custody on the 2006 census date—representing 65 percent of all offenders held, with black youth accounting for 40 percent of the juvenile custody population.

* Nationally, the custody rate was highest for black youth and lowest for Asian youth. For every 100,000 black juveniles living in the United States, 767 were in custody in a juvenile facility on the 2006 census date; the rate was 540 for American Indians, 326 for Hispanic youth, 170 for Whites, and 85 for Asians.

* The overall juvenile custody population decreased 11 percent between 2001 and 2006. The decline for white youth was 21 percent, double the rate of minority youth, which declined by 8 percent.

Deaths in Custody

The death rate for youth in custody is lower than that for youth in the general population, and OJJDP's latest data indicate that deaths of juveniles in custody are relatively rare. According to the 2004 JRFC, 27 youth died while in custody in juvenile facilities compared with 26 in 2002, 30 in 2000, and 44 in 1994. Suicide was the leading cause of death according to the 2004 census, accounting for 16 deaths while 5 deaths resulted from illness or other natural causes, 4 from accidents, and 2 from homicides. The death rate was generally higher for private than for public facilities.

Juvenile offenders in custody, 2006

Race/ethnicity	Number	Percent	Percent change 2001–2006
Total	92,854	100	-11
White	32,495	35	-21
Minority	60,359	65	-4
Black	37,337	40	-8
Hispanic	19,027	20	6
Amer. Indian	1,828	2	-16
Asian	1,155	1	-23
Other/mixed	1,012	1	63

Note: Detail may not total 100% because of rounding.

Online Resources

Most of the data in this section were taken from OJJDP's online Statistical Briefing Book (discussed earlier in this chapter). Detailed information on juvenile corrections is also available in *Juvenile Offenders and Victims: 2006 National Report*. The custody chapter of the *National Report* includes detailed information about detained and committed juvenile offenders, residents' time in placement, security features of facilities, overcrowding, substance abuse screening, and sexual violence in facilities. To access these resources, visit the OJJDP Web site at www.ojp.usdoj.gov/ojjdp and click on the "Statistics" section.

APPENDIXES

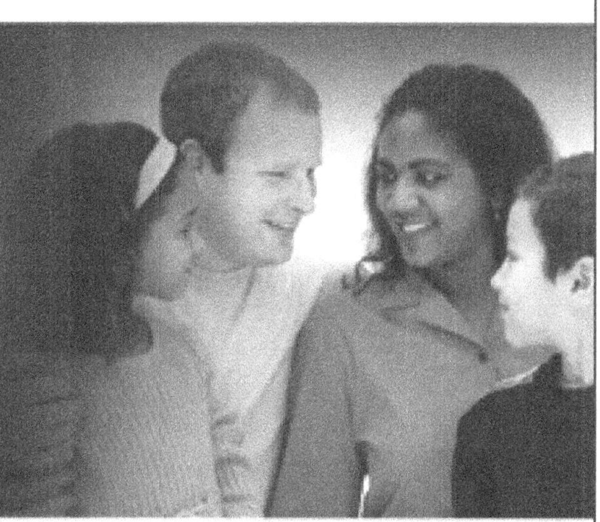

APPENDIX A
OJJDP Organization

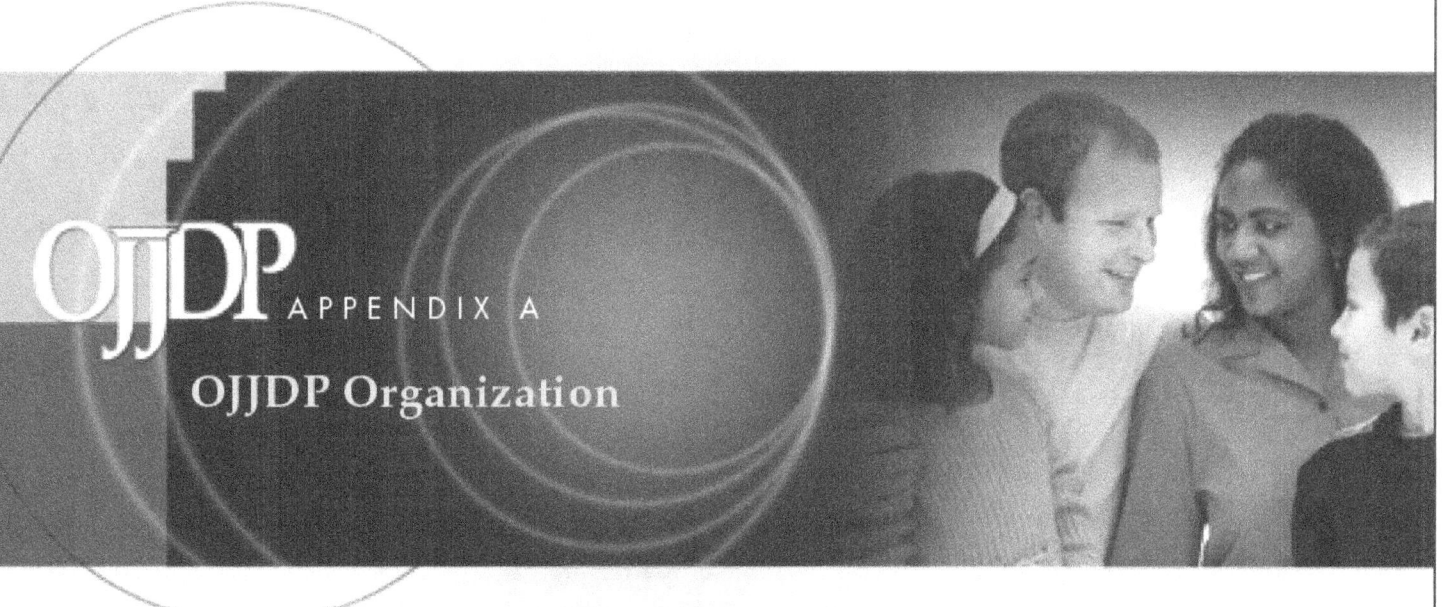

Office of Juvenile Justice and Delinquency Prevention

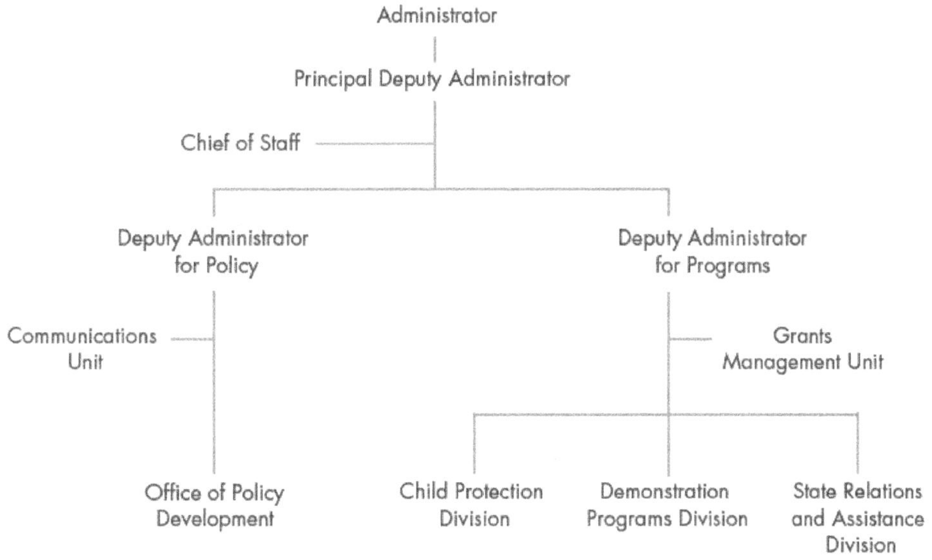

OJJDP Office of the Administrator

The Office of the Administrator (OA) establishes OJJDP's priorities and policies, oversees the management of the Office's divisions, and fosters collaboration with Federal, State, and local agencies and associations that share OJJDP's commitment to preventing and combating juvenile delinquency and addressing the problem of missing and exploited children.

Office of Policy Development

The Office of Policy Development (OPD) assists the OJJDP Administrator in coordinating national policy on juvenile justice. OPD advises the Administrator on policy and legal issues and

how OJJDP can best accomplish its mission. OPD also provides leadership and direction for OJJDP's research and training and technical assistance efforts and oversees the agency's communications and planning activities.

Communications Unit

The Communications Unit (CU) is responsible for OJJDP's information dissemination and outreach. CU develops OJJDP publications, manages its Web site and online services, and performs a range of writing and editing functions to support the office. CU also serves as a liaison to OJP on media-related issues.

Child Protection Division

The Child Protection Division (CPD) develops and administers programs related to crimes against children and children's exposure to violence. It provides leadership and funding in the areas of enforcement, intervention, and prevention. CPD's activities include supporting programs that promote effective policies and procedures to respond to the problems of missing and exploited children, Internet crimes against children, abused and neglected children, and children exposed to domestic or community violence.

Demonstration Programs Division

The Demonstration Programs Division (DPD) provides funds to public and private agencies, organizations, and individuals to develop and support programs and replicate tested approaches to delinquency prevention, treatment, and control in areas such as mentoring, substance abuse, gangs, truancy, chronic juvenile offending, and community-based sanctions. DPD also supports and coordinates efforts with tribal governments to expand and improve tribal juvenile justice systems and develop programs and policies that address problems facing tribal youth.

State Relations and Assistance Division

The State Relations and Assistance Division (SRAD) provides funds to help State and local governments achieve the system improvement goals of the JJDP Act, combat underage drinking, implement delinquency prevention programs, address disproportionate minority contact, and support initiatives to hold juvenile offenders accountable for their actions. SRAD also supports and coordinates community efforts to identify and respond to critical juvenile justice and delinquency prevention needs.

Grants Management Unit

The Grants Management Unit (GMU) provides grant administration assistance and guidance to OJJDP's program divisions. GMU also provides technical assistance and support for grant application and award activities to OJJDP staff and constituents.

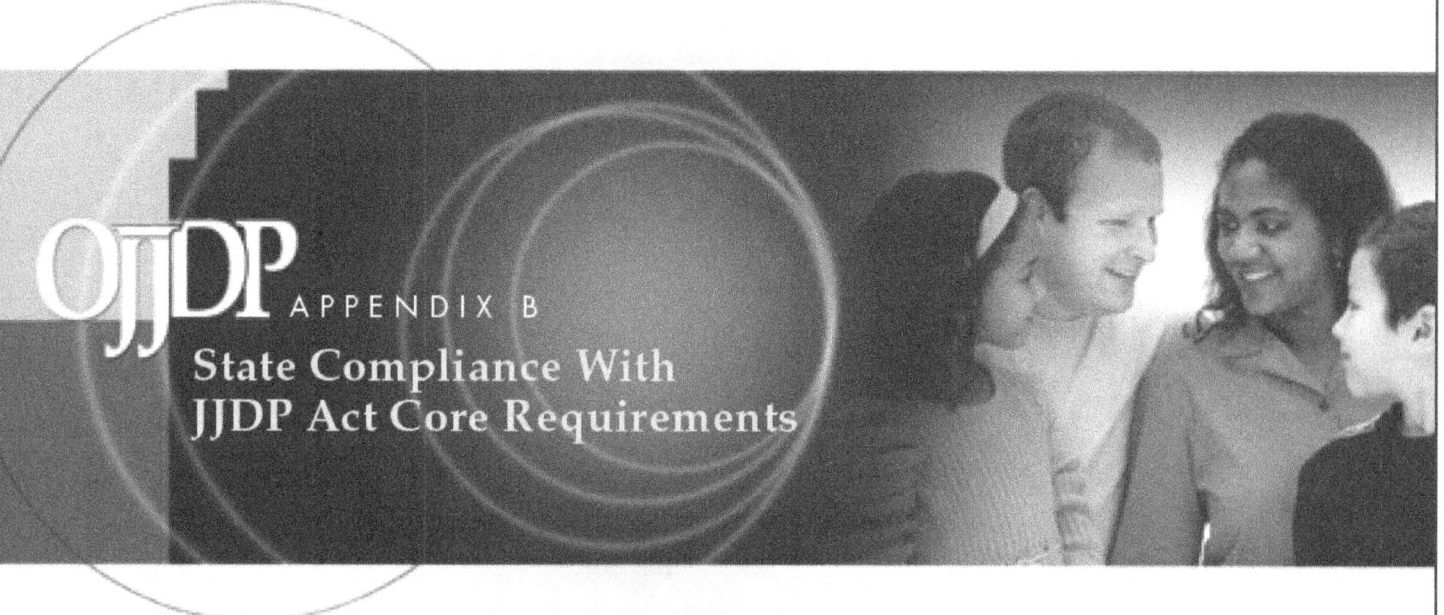

OJJDP APPENDIX B
State Compliance With JJDP Act Core Requirements

The status reported in this summary is current as of November 2006. Deinstitutionalization of status offenders, separation, and jail/lockup removal compliance are based on 2004 State monitoring reports. Disproportionate minority contact compliance is based on FY 2006 Formula Grants program comprehensive plans. Wyoming did not participate in the FY 2006 or FY 2007 Formula Grants program.

Section 223(a)(11): Deinstitutionalization of Status Offenders and Nonoffenders (DSO)

Full compliance—zero violations: American Samoa, Maine.

Full compliance—*de minimis* exceptions:[a] Alabama, Alaska, Arizona, Arkansas, California, Colorado, Connecticut, Delaware, District of Columbia, Florida, Georgia, Guam, Hawaii, Idaho, Illinois, Indiana, Iowa, Kansas, Kentucky, Louisiana, Maryland, Massachusetts, Michigan, Minnesota, Missouri, Montana, Nebraska, Nevada, New Hampshire, New Jersey, New Mexico, New York, North Carolina, North Dakota, Ohio, Oklahoma, Oregon, Pennsylvania, Puerto Rico, Rhode Island, South Carolina, South Dakota, Tennessee, Texas, Utah, Vermont, Virginia, West Virginia.

Not in compliance: Mississippi, Northern Mariana Islands, Washington, Wisconsin, Virgin Islands.

---

[a] Fewer than 29.4 violations per 100,000 persons under age 18 in the State.

Section 223(a)(12): Separation of Juveniles and Adult Offenders

Full compliance—zero violations: Alabama, Alaska, American Samoa, Arizona, Arkansas, California, Colorado, Connecticut, Delaware, District of Columbia, Florida, Georgia, Hawaii, Idaho, Illinois, Indiana, Iowa, Kentucky, Maine, Maryland, Massachusetts, Minnesota, Mississippi, Montana, Nebraska, Nevada, New Hampshire, New Mexico, North Dakota, Ohio, Oklahoma, Pennsylvania, Rhode Island, South Carolina, Tennessee, Texas, Utah, Vermont, Washington, West Virginia, Wisconsin.

Full compliance—exception provision:[b] Guam, Kansas, Louisiana, Michigan, Missouri, New Jersey, New York, North Carolina, Oregon, South Dakota, Virginia.

Not in compliance: Northern Mariana Islands, Puerto Rico, Virgin Islands.

Section 223(a)(14): Jail and Lockup Removal

Full compliance—zero violations: Alabama, American Samoa, District of Columbia, Idaho, Illinois, Kentucky, New Mexico.

Full compliance—de minimis exceptions:[c] Alaska, Arizona, Arkansas, California, Colorado, Connecticut, Delaware, Florida, Georgia, Guam, Hawaii, Indiana, Iowa, Kansas, Louisiana, Maine, Maryland, Massachusetts, Michigan, Minnesota, Missouri, Montana, Nebraska, Nevada, New Hampshire, New Jersey, New York, North Carolina, North Dakota, Ohio, Oklahoma, Pennsylvania, Rhode Island, South Dakota, Tennessee, Texas, Utah, Vermont, Virginia, Washington, West Virginia, Wisconsin.

Not in compliance: Mississippi, Northern Mariana Islands, Oregon, Puerto Rico, South Carolina, Virgin Islands.

Section 223(a)(22): Disproportionate Minority Contact (DMC)

In compliance: Alabama, Alaska, American Samoa, Arizona, Arkansas, California, Colorado, Connecticut, Delaware, District of Columbia, Florida, Georgia, Guam, Hawaii, Idaho, Illinois, Indiana, Iowa, Kansas, Kentucky, Louisiana, Maine, Maryland, Massachusetts, Michigan, Minnesota, Missouri, Montana, Nebraska, Nevada, New Hampshire, New Jersey, New Mexico, New York, North Carolina, North Dakota, Ohio, Oklahoma, Oregon, Pennsylvania, Rhode

---

[b] OJJDP regulatory criteria set forth in Section 31.303(f)(6)(ii) of the OJJDP Formula Grants Regulations (28 C.F.R. 31), published in the May 31, 1995, *Federal Register,* allow States reporting noncompliant incidents to continue in the program provided the incidents are not in violation of State law and no pattern or practice exists.

[c] State was found in compliance on the basis of numerical or substantive *de minimis* standard criteria set forth in Section 31.303(f)(6)(iii)(B) of the OJJDP Formula Grants Regulations (28 C.F.R. 31) and published in the May 31, 1995, *Federal Register.*

Island, South Carolina, South Dakota, Tennessee, Texas, Utah, Vermont, Virginia, Washington, West Virginia, Virgin Islands, Wisconsin.

Not in compliance: Mississippi, Northern Mariana Islands.

Exempt from DMC requirement (racially homogeneous population): Puerto Rico.

Compliance Summary Totals
(as of November 21, 2006)

Requirement and Compliance Status	Number of Jurisdictions
Deinstitutionalization of Status Offenders (DSO)	
Full compliance—zero violations	2
Full compliance—*de minimis* exceptions	48
Not in compliance	5
Separation of Juvenile and Adult Offenders	
Full compliance—zero violations	41
Full compliance—exception provision	11
Not in compliance	3
Jail and Lockup Removal	
Full compliance—zero violations	7
Full compliance—*de minimis* exceptions	42
Not in compliance	6
Disproportionate Minority Contact (DMC)	
In compliance	52
Not in compliance	2
Exempt from DMC requirement	1

Note: States' eligibility to receive FY 2007 formula grants was determined on the basis of 2004 monitoring reports for compliance with JJDP Act core requirements regarding DSO, separation, and jail and lockup removal and on the basis of information in FY 2006 Formula Grants Program comprehensive plans for compliance with the DMC core requirement. One State did not participate in the FY 2007 Formula Grants Program.

www.ingramcontent.com/pod-product-compliance
Lightning Source LLC
Chambersburg PA
CBHW080322290526
45790CB00005B/2148